God and His Children

Learning about prayer through Christians in discussion

Tom Holland

God and His Children by Tom Holland
First Published by Apiary Publishing Ltd 2017

Apiary Publishing Ltd
71-75 Shelton St
London WC2H 9JQ

enquiries@apiarypublishing.com

British Library Cataloguing-in-Publication Data

A catalogue record for this book is available from the British Library

ISBN: 978-1-912445-05-9

Preface

The thoughts reflected in the following pages are not intended to provide pat answers—indeed, they probably raise more questions than they answer. I have written in narrative form because I know that some find reading difficult, particularly abstract ideas, difficult. I hope that this format will enable readers to see the practical issues associated with praying.

Throughout my life there have always been people who have challenged and inspired me. This book is dedicated to them, many of whom will never know what their example has meant.

The characters in the first chapter of the book were suggested by Heather Brown. I am grateful to her for her creative suggestions. These are the people who the remaining chapters follow as they consider the all-important theme of prayer.

Book Reviews

Tom Holland brings to this book the wisdom of a long-serving minister, the heart of a caring pastor, and the knowledge of an internationally respected theologian. That is a very rare combination and no subject is better served by it than a discussion of prayer. In these pages you will discover not only profound truth simply explained but answers to the questions we have all asked when struggling to pray. - **Rev. Phil Hill BA, MPhil, Pastoral and Church Theologian, Wales Evangelical School of Theology**

Tom Holland asks the right questions and thereby primes the pump for an eminently readable, engaging and informative reflection on the practice of prayer. All readers, whatever their spiritual maturity, will find much to stimulate their thinking and better equip them to pray. - **Dr Lawson Murray, President - Scripture Union Canada.**

The book deals with many questions about prayer, constantly asked by Christians; for instance, 'Why pray when God is sovereign? 'What about healing?' 'Since Jesus said "I do not pray for the world", should we pray for unbelievers?' All in all helpful, unusual and not without challenge for believers at every stage, although particularly helpful for those young in age and spiritual maturity. - **Philip Grist in The Evangelical Times**

This is a unique book. Its teaching on prayer through dialogue makes it an easy and fast-paced read that proves challenging to one's prayer life. And the characters bring to it a pastoral reality, as issues such as parenthood, bereavement, healing, and personal evangelism are dealt with. A great little aid for all of us who wrestle in prayer. - **Natalie Brand, writer and mother**

With questions for group discussion

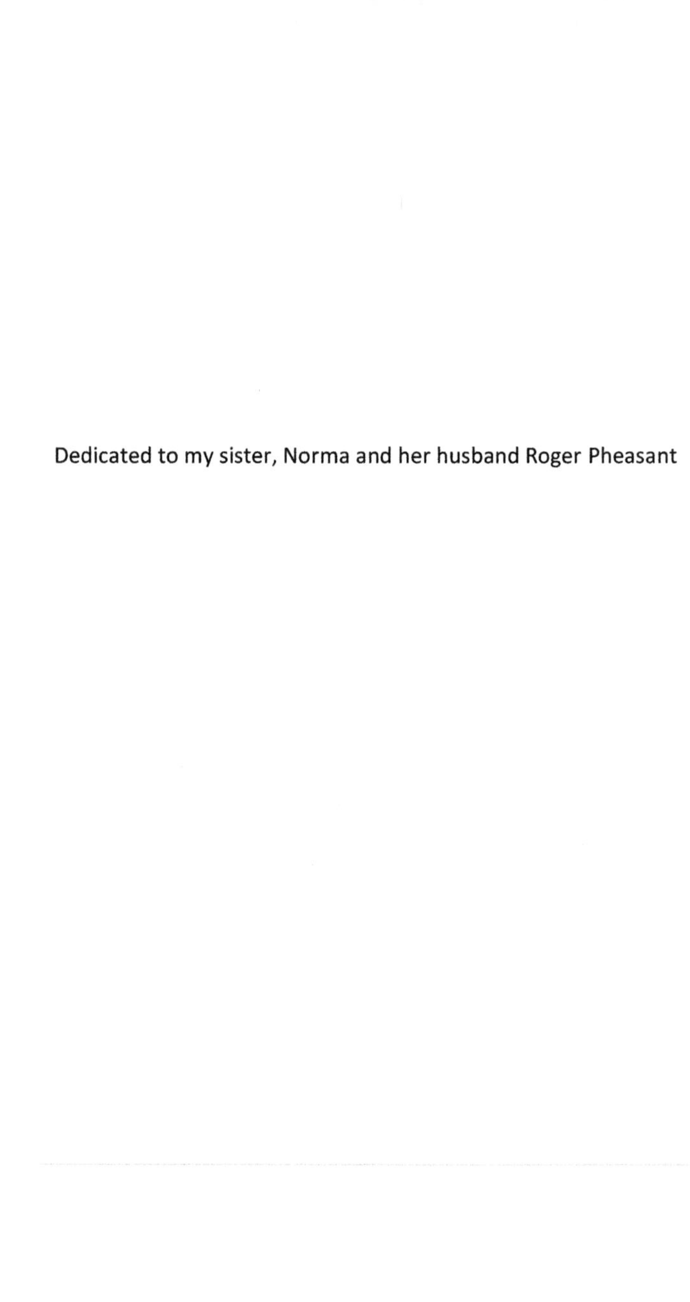

Dedicated to my sister, Norma and her husband Roger Pheasant

Contents

Getting it Straight

Prayer and the Sovereignty of God

'Hello, Dave; nice to see you. Come in out of the cold.'

The tall young man stepped out of the freezing darkness of the late January night into the bright hall of Jim Thompson's house on the outskirts of town.

'Go in the front room and take your coat off. Tea or coffee?'

'Oh! tea, please.'

'OK, won't be a moment.'

Dave went into the room and a blazing log fire immediately warmed him. It was in welcome contrast to the sub-zero temperature outside. He began to take his coat off, still flecked with snow, and sat in the rocking chair near the fire. He felt it would take all evening to thaw out.

Jim came in with an old log-basket full of wood and put it down on the hearth. 'I thought you might not make it tonight with that wretched asthma of yours.'

'I must admit, I was nearly at the point of phoning to cancel; but I really want to talk this matter over with you, Jim. It's been bothering me a great deal.'

'Yes, I was interested in your comment as you left on Sunday. You said you'd been confused by what Tom, a Christian friend at work, had been saying about "true" prayer?'

'That's right.'

Dave stretched out his long legs to the hearth and let out a short sigh. He'd got on quite well with Tom when the young engineer had first joined the firm. He'd become a Christian during his final year at college, and Dave had been encouraged at the thought of having a like-minded colleague. But recently his appreciation had been slowly waning. The two men had begun to differ on a number of issues, particularly prayer. In the past, Dave had always stood his ground, sometimes at great cost, when his faith in Christ had been challenged. Now he felt threatened in a different way, and he hardly knew how to handle his feelings or thoughts.

'Tom's views on prayer are so different from what you've said on Sunday evenings. I've been left not knowing what to believe.'

'In what way do our views differ?'

Dave sighed again, a slightly wheezy sigh. He was feeling warmer now and very glad to have the chance to air his problem.

'Perhaps,' he began slowly, 'the best way I can explain it is ... well ... Tom is so fantastically optimistic about prayer and what it will achieve. He hardly talks of anything else when he's not working, and sometimes even when he is! He seems to think anything is to be had for the asking, quoting Scripture to prove it; whereas you're, well, more ...'

'Cautious?' Jim interjected.

'Well, yes. I don't mean to offend you, Jim, but Tom seems so sure God is going to answer his prayers and that he has a right to expect Him to do so; but you're, well, not quite so encouraging.'

Jim smiled across from his beloved old arm chair. He understood Dave's dilemma, perhaps better than the young man would ever know. He was glad he'd come to talk it over and hoped he could help. Jim had a particular concern for Dave. He was a hard-working young man and a keen Christian, but life hadn't been easy as he'd always wrestled with asthma. However, now he was married to Becky, and they were expecting their first baby.

Just as Jim got up to put another log on the fire the door opened, and Jo, his wife, came in with two steaming mugs of tea.

'Ah, great! Thanks love. Here we are, Dave.'

'How's Becky?'

'A bit tired, but not as sick as she has been. She's very well most of the time, thanks Jo,' the proud father-to-be answered, with a grin.

She turned to Jim, 'I'm just popping across to see if Mrs Edwards is OK, I'll leave you two men in peace.'

The two men sipped their tea in silence for a few moments, and then Jim asked, 'What kind of things does your friend pray about?'

'Oh, practically everything! He'll pray he'll have good weather when he goes on holiday; or if he wants something, say a car, he'll pray that God will give it to him—the right colour, price, everything!'

'And does he get these things?'

Dave shrugged his shoulders a little. 'Seems he does. He says he does. And there are other things. He claims that anyone who asks for a particular marriage partner or a particular job will get them. Then there's the question of healing.'

'Healing? Go on.'

Dave shifted in his chair and looked away from Jim for a moment, gazing into the flames that were leaping up from the logs.

'Yes, healing. He reckons that if I had more faith and asked more boldly, that ... well ... that I could be rid of my asthma.'

'I see.'

'He keeps on about it. Didn't I believe that God wanted to heal me? Did I think that a God of love would keep me suffering unnecessarily? All I had to do was claim healing in the name of Jesus, and I would get it. He offered to pray and lay hands on me.'

'And did he?'

'No, no ... I needed time to think. I wasn't sure; and, as I said, you were preaching something quite different on Sundays. The two views didn't square up. That's why I wanted to see you to talk about them.'

'I take it you're thinking particularly about my sermon on God being a sovereign God?'

'Yes; and your emphasis that He has the last word, as it were, on whether or not we get what we ask for. You say it's up to Him whether our prayers are answered, whereas Tom claims that if we ask in faith we'll receive everything we ask.'

'And he can't point to a single occasion when he didn't get what he asked?'

Thoroughly warmed now and refreshed by the tea, Dave felt very much at home and at ease. It was a relief to be bringing his thoughts out into the open, and he decided he had nothing to lose by laying all the facts before his Pastor.

'To be frank, Jim, I think there have been times, but he won't say it in so many words. I know for a fact that a lady who was brought to his healing group died a few weeks later, and the parents of a little girl, who was very ill—I think with meningitis—really believed and trusted she would recover, but she didn't. It was awful. The parents were devastated and felt that God had let them down. That must have been like the knife turning in the wound.'

'Yes, I heard about the family. It rather takes the wind out of your friend's sails, doesn't it?'

'Mmm. The trouble is though, if God is sovereign …'

'… why bother to pray?' Jim said in anticipation.

'Exactly! If God's will is going to be done anyway, what's the point of praying?'

'Yes, well, both views do present their own set of problems.'

'You mean your position raises some difficult questions too?'

'Only if you misunderstand it,' said Jim, 'and I fear it is easy to misunderstand.'

'How do you mean?'

'Well, let me put it this way: I think what you're saying is that because I tend to emphasise God's sovereignty, you doubt the value of asking Him anything; but you're not convinced by friend's position as he's forever making claims that don't always get realised. His faith seems very attractive on the surface, but when you look closely, it doesn't always work out as he says. It must be very difficult for him to be really honest about prayer.'

'The problem's obviously not new to you!' smiled Dave. 'Have others been to see you about this?'

'No, not recently; but I know a little about it from my own experience. I've been the same way and had to sort out the same thoughts.' There was something in Jim's eyes that made Dave feel he'd better not ask any further.

'I must say I'm relieved! I was afraid you might think I didn't have enough faith or that my motives were wrong.'

'Not at all! There are many areas in which we never stop learning and growing. In fact, I'll hazard a guess you were beginning to think I was the one lacking in faith compared to Tom.'

'You've read my thoughts exactly!' exclaimed Dave, grinning broadly and warming to his Pastor's insight.

'I think I can help you, Dave—in fact, I'm sure I can! But the whole matter of prayer is far too big an issue to get clear in just one evening.'

Jim picked up his ipad from the table by his chair, opened it and turned to the diary.

'What I think we'll do tonight is outline some basic principles on this matter of sovereignty—we need to get this clear before we get down to talking about prayer. Let's see; I'll book next Tuesday evening—after that, we may have to get together as and when opportunities arise. Is that OK?'

'Great! It's very kind of you to spare the time. Are you sure you're not too busy?'

'First things first,' said Jim, slipping the ipad back on the table. 'I think if we can get these issues sorted out it'll be very worthwhile. You could bring Becky with you if you like and any of your friends who've got similar problems.'

'Thanks, that's a great idea. I can think of a few already.'

At that moment, they heard footsteps coming up the drive. Jo was back, but judging from the time she was taking to open the front door, it seemed the lock was stuck.

'Oh no,' Jim grimaced, guiltily, 'the lock's frozen again. I'll just let her in.'

He crossed the room quickly just as she tapped on the window and called out.

'Have to put a spot of oil on it,' said Jim returning, slapping his own wrist. Both men laughed. 'Now where were we?'

'You said you'd tackle the question of God's sovereignty. But what exactly do you mean by sovereignty? It seems to mean different things to different people. Do you mean that every detail and event in our lives is predetermined by Him?'

Jim settled back in his chair and pushed one of the logs on the fire with his foot. It immediately responded with a burst of hot crackling flame, accompanied by a gust of smoke, which made Dave cough. Jim apologised for his thoughtlessness, but his young friend assured him he was quite alright and eager to hear what he had to say.

'No, I don't believe everything is predetermined. If it was, we wouldn't be free or responsible people—and we're clearly given many areas of responsibility and the freedom to make decisions.'

'For example?'

'Well, we're free to marry, to try for a family and, if we have children, to bring them up the way we choose. We're free to change our jobs or move house if we wish—although, as Christians, we'd pray and think carefully about such things. We could hardly claim that everything that happens to us was a result of divine decree.'

'Yes, I think I see. You mean that God gives us freedom to make these choices ourselves—they aren't preordained from the beginning of time. So what areas is He sovereign over?'

Jim leaned forward, resting his forearms on his knees and clasping his hands. The expression on his face changed slightly as he thought carefully how to answer Dave's question.

'I'd have to put salvation at the top of the list. From its beginning to its end, salvation is the result of God's sovereignty. Then He's sovereign in human history, and thirdly—the area you're most concerned about—He's sovereign in prayer.'

Jim was conscious of a querying look in Dave's eyes, which prompted him to pause.

'Am I going too fast?

'You're making assumptions that I need some help with. Of course, I accept what you say; but you're creating holes in my understanding that my convictions are leaking through!'

'I tell you what, Dave, let's say we keep God's sovereignty in salvation for another time—it's too big a subject to handle now. What do you say we spend a little time tonight on God's sovereignty in history and in prayer?'

'That's fine by me! But do you mean sovereignty in the sense that all history will eventually serve His purpose, or in a detailed sense, that He's responsible for everyone and everything?'

'I mean both! It's clearly the message of Scripture that the wrath of man will ultimately praise God. He's Lord of lords and King of kings, and every knee will bow to Him. You know, of course, God called the pagan king Cyrus "my servant," and that godless governors and magistrates are also described as His servants? Not every decision they made or make reflects God's will or character, but they will, eventually, fulfil His purpose.'

'Because it's taught in Scripture, I'll accept that,' Dave said, cautiously, 'but it's a difficult teaching to accept when you think of some rulers, isn't it?'

'I agree. So much confronting us suggests God's not sovereign; but, when we look back through history, we see time and again how He overturned the plans and deeds of evil people to bring eventual blessing. And, of course, much of Scripture states this.'

'But how about His sovereignty in my life? Is He responsible for every detail?'

'It is a difficult one to answer! In as much as He could break in and perform miracles to change its natural course, there is an element in which He is responsible. But miracles aren't there to provide escape routes from problems; in no way does the Bible teach that—that's why they're relatively rare.'

'Then, in what way is He sovereign over my life?'

'Well, as I've said, in salvation; but He's also sovereign over the whole of your life in a bigger way than orchestrating little details that would stop you being a free agent. I once thought God was directly responsible for everything, but I found I was making Him the author of evil—for children being abused and bullied, for adultery and marriage break ups, for rapes, murders, famines, wars, and so on. It was ridiculous! I was attributing to Him what the Bible ascribes to Satan.'

'I see what you mean,' Dave replied. 'So how did you adjust your understanding?'

'Well, I searched the Scriptures more carefully, and came to the conclusion that God's not responsible for all my circumstances but is unconditionally responsible for *me* in my circumstances. That's where I think the biblical harmony lies.'

'Are you saying that God is left impotent when I'm suffering—that He can only comfort me and eventually get me to heaven?'

'No, but neither do I see, as I once did, that all the details of my life are of His making—predetermined by Him. He makes them serve His purpose, but He's not necessarily responsible for all of them.'

'But am I at the mercy of events He doesn't control?'

'No! He can and does set all the limits—the story of Job shows that. But setting the limits doesn't mean being responsible for the detail!'

Just then the door opened, and Jo put her head round. 'I don't want to interrupt you two men,' she said, 'but I think you ought to know it's snowing heavily and its going to continue for the next six hours,

The drive's frozen up, Jim, so you won't be able to run Dave home. Perhaps you ought to watch the time.'

'Thanks, love. Do you want to go now, Dave?'

He thought for a moment, aware that Becky would be worried; but the conversation and roaring log fire were so tempting that Dave decided to stay.

'I'll just text Becky to check she's OK. I'd like to finish off this subject, if that's alright?'

'Fine by me,' said Jim. 'While you do that, I'll organise some more tea.'

Soon the two men were back in conversation and Jo brought in another tray of tea. This time she stayed to enjoy their company and the warmth of the roaring fire.

'Are the girls alright?'

'Yes, I've just taken them a drink up. Sophie's helping Emma with her maths homework. Mum's obviously not good enough!'

'Well, where were we, Dave?' said Jim, 'How far did we get?'

'You've talked about God being sovereign in history. You said you'd deal with His sovereignty in salvation at another time,' replied Dave.

'Ah, yes. Well, that brings us on to prayer.'

'And this is the heart of my problem,' responded Dave. 'If God is sovereign, especially in answering prayer, won't it be the same whether I pray or not?'

'I can understand where you're coming from; but you're concentrating on one aspect of truth, and the

Bible gives a much fuller picture. It's like light. It's possible to break it up into its spectrum and examine its constituents, but it's only white, or true, when all the constituents are blended together.'

'Is this what you mean when you talk of paradox?' queried Jo.

'That's right! Paradox is truth that seems incompatible, like man's responsibility and God's sovereignty—they're apparently conflicting truths that must be held together.'

'I must confess,' she replied, 'I tend to think that claiming something's a paradox is a sort of theological accounting method to keep the books straight. You know, a sort of short cut!'

Jim laughed. 'It's your accountancy training coming out again!'

'Actually, I don't find any problem with it,' Dave interrupted.

'You don't?'

'No, Jo. Paradoxes aren't only in biblical truths, they crop up everywhere, even in science,' he said, reassuring her that it was no sleight-of-hand trickery to get rid of a problem. 'I am told that physicists have observed that light sometimes behaves as if it consisted of particles and yet at other times as a wave—as a result the characteristics of light can only be properly described by a theory which holds both of these ideas together.'

'Well, that's interesting,' said Jim, 'because this is exactly how it is with biblical paradox. I didn't realise it had the approval of the scientists though!'

Dave smiled knowingly. 'Jim, you've mentioned the truth of God's sovereignty in prayer; I think I can predict what you're now going to tell me is on the other side of the coin—what the apparently conflicting truth is. Please go on, and I'll see if I'm right!'

'Well, on the other side of the coin are all the statements, exhortations, commands and examples of prayer.' Dave smiled in agreement. 'This is where I keep my eyes on Jesus and the apostles. Even though they clearly rested in the reality of God's sovereignty, they couldn't help but pray. It was natural to them. In fact, it was impossible for them to obey, to serve or witness without committing themselves and their work to God.'

'Do you think we should keep the whole of the Bible's teaching and the early Christians' practice in balance when we consider any truth?'

'Absolutely! If we don't keep them in harmony, we could easily drift into something that's different from the early believers' experience. We must never be fatalistic because that removes all sense of responsibility. But, equally, we mustn't become activists, believing that all God's work depends on us. That would limit Him to the whims of our willingness to obey and serve. Both are wrong.'

'Well, thanks a lot, Jim,' said Dave, glancing over at the clock. 'You've given me plenty to chew over before next week.'

'Good! But just one final thing: even when our prayers couldn't have a bearing on the outcome of events, we should still pray.'

'But what would be the point, other than going through a ritual? You don't mean that, do you?'

'Not at all! Some of the most important aspects of prayer are worship, praise and thanksgiving. So, even if you continued to have difficulty in reconciling God's sovereignty with man's responsibility, His sovereignty would, or should, heighten these very important aspects of prayer.'

Dave smiled. 'That's something I'd never thought of. It's certainly given me food for thought.'

'I'll get your coat, Dave,' Jo said. 'You'll find it very slippery underfoot, so be careful how you go.'

Questions to Ponder

1. John thought that the two views he had heard clashed. What teaching on the same subject leaves a similar sense of tension? Has anyone been able to help you to resolve the problem?
2. What does Christian freedom mean? What are the areas of your life in which you conscious of lacking freedom?

3. Why was Dave concerned with Tom's view of prayer. Was his concern justified? Whatever you decided, justify your answer.
4. Dave's circumstances and personality caused him to see differently from Tom. What do you think Dave had to cope with that Tom does not seem to have experienced.
5. What had David resorted to in order to answer his questions? Have you ever done a similar thing and if so did it help?
6. How did Dave feel about Tom's claims?
7. What was Dave's big issue concerning prayer? Has it ever troubled you and if so, how did you resolve it?
8. How does Dave define God's sovereignty—do you think he was right? Reflect on your answer and consider to what extent it may be biased or to what extent it is genuinely based on biblical teaching.

The Right to Demand

Prayer and Healing

Jim opened the front door, holding his mobile to his ear, 'Hello Dave,' he whispered, 'go through to the lounge, I'll be with you in a few minutes.'

Closing the front door behind him, Dave walked through the hall and opened the door of the lounge. He stood, warming himself by the fire. His thinking was beginning to clarify since his last visit, especially as he and Becky had spent a few hours together one evening going through the passages that Jim had written down. He was beginning to see how dangerous it was to overemphasise one truth at the cost of another.

'Good,' said Jim as he returned to the lounge, his hand stretched out towards Dave. 'That was Simon. He was telling me his Dad's feeling much better after his operation last week.'

'That's fantastic,' beamed Dave. 'They said it was very doubtful whether he'd pull through. Do you think it was an answer to ...'

'Prayer? Yes, I do!'

'Actually, Jim, I was wondering if you would mind if we talked over the matter of prayer and healing tonight. Tom's been very excited about someone who went forward at a meeting last week and testified he'd been healed.'

'What was his problem?'

'Cancer. He'd been given only three months to live. He's convinced he's been healed.'

'Well, I hope he's right. Have a seat, Dave. I think you became attached to the rocking chair last week! Make yourself comfortable and I'll see if I can improve the fire without wrapping you up in smoke!' Dave laughed as he remembered the sudden gust of pungent smoke that had engulfed him the week before.

'Well, you've certainly chosen a good subject for tonight! Rather than talking generally about people we know, let's try to keep to what Scripture says.'

'That's the whole problem for me. Tom seems to have so much scriptural support—I feel as though I'm arguing against the evidence all the time.'

'I know what you mean; but be careful. Keep in mind that it's not the evidence you question but his interpretation of it.'

'I hadn't seen it quite that way before. Come to think of it, Tom's keenness has been so infectious that I've almost assumed he was presenting the truth. Rejecting what he says has felt like rejecting what God could do if I were less suspicious and gave myself totally.'

'Ah! There's a danger there,' Jim said. 'If by that you mean give yourself totally to God, then that's what we must be doing daily. But if you mean give yourself wholly to Tom's views, treating all your doubts as unbelief, then you could be opening yourself up to dangers to which, sadly, many have fallen prey.'

'In what way?'

'Well, we mustn't think reason is automatically an enemy of faith. It's an enemy when God is left out; but when God is included—when all that He has said and promised becomes part of the reasoning—it's not an enemy, but a friend that gives tremendous support. We're constantly invited to use our reasoning by the biblical writers.'[1]

'I see,' responded Dave. 'So you don't think it's unbelief when I to want to think things through and be satisfied in my mind?'

'Not at all—as long as God is at the centre of your thinking. Tom might be right; and if he is, you must listen to him. But if he's wrong, you must pray for him, because at some point he's going to get badly hurt.'

'There doesn't seem to be room for that possibility in his thinking!'

'And that's why he's in so much danger. Can I ask you what the "evidence" is that Tom has given?'

The question didn't really need to be asked. Jim had the texts at his fingertips, but thought it would help Dave to articulate his own concerns.

'Well, he pointed out that Jesus healed all the sick that came to Him and gave His disciples authority to heal the sick as well, and to command demons to come out of people.'

'Yes,' said Jim, 'and I suppose he'd say it's only the absence of faith that stops the same thing happening today.'

'That's right,' said Dave, glancing over to the fire—his attention attracted by a spark that had jumped from the licking flames and had landed on the hearth.

Jim sighed deeply as though his emotions had overcome him. Dave looked up from the fire and saw his eyes As soon as Dave looked over, Jim forced a smile in an attempt to cover the obvious distress he was in. His voice broke through the lump that had come to his throat, but within a syllable or two it was back to normal.

'You mean in Nazareth? But that is Tom's point. Jesus couldn't do miracles there because of their unbelief.'[2]

'That's true, but I wasn't thinking of that occasion. I was thinking of the pool of Bethesda, in John 5.[3] Did you know that it measured 160 x 480 feet and its edge was crowded with people who wanted to be healed? Yet Jesus healed only one out of what must have been many hundreds of sick people.'

'But didn't Jesus command His disciples to go and heal the sick?'[4]

'Yes he did, and, of course, they did. But again, not everybody was healed. Paul seems to have known an ongoing sickness[5] and Timothy was advised to take wine for his stomach's sake.[6] Paul refers to his regular sicknesses, and he even had to leave one of his companions sick while he continued on his missionary tour.[7] He also had to send a sick colleague home from missionary work.'[8]

'But you wouldn't deny that the apostles healed the sick, would you?'

'No, of course not; but I'd have to question anyone's claim that it was a lack of faith, or even some sin, that was the cause of people not being healed. As I've said, members of the apostolic band experienced sickness, without any suggestion that they felt out of God's will or were somehow responsible for their condition. Remember what we saw last week: we must keep the Scripture's teaching and practice in harmony. If we leave any evidence out, we aren't being honest and won't finish up with a true reflection of biblical truth.'

'But ... well, Tom says that the passage in Matthew 8 verse 17—where Matthew quotes from Isaiah that Jesus took up our infirmities and carried our diseases—shows that healing is available for all in the death of Jesus.'

'He's right, it is! And that is what Paul says in Romans 8. But he makes it clear that that's only going to happen when Jesus returns. Then, our weak bodies will be made like His glorious or resurrected body!'[9]

'So, you don't agree with Tom that it's available now?'

'No, not to the extent he does. I don't. God does graciously grant some tokens of his power to be available now; and at such times it is as if the power of the coming age has broken into time. But the fact is that to a great extent we must all live with pain and suffering until Jesus returns ... you can read 1

Corinthians 15 and the middle of Romans 8 to see what will happen then.'[10]

'Can I just check you out again, Jim? You *do* believe people really are healed today?'

'Yes, of course.'

'But you just don't believe people can *demand* healing?'

'Correct again!'

'Do you deny that healing can occur on a "mass" scale?'

'No, I don't deny that. When there's been an outpouring of God's Spirit the miraculous is almost natural, but never worked up. What I'd be inclined to deny are claims that such times of visitation are presently being experienced in the UK. They may well be happening in some other parts of the world, but I see little evidence that this is happening in the West today—although I wish such were truly the case! But remember, even the apostles didn't live continually in such an experience—an honest reading of the whole of Acts shows that.'

'When will there be an outpouring, then?'

'We've come back to what we talked about last week! God is sovereign, and we must never lose sight of this.'

Dave smiled, but it was obvious that he still didn't feel convinced.

'You're not sure, are you, Dave? Do you think Tom might be right?'

'Not right, but I do think he has a sort of cornerstone. What you've said makes sense, apart from the fact that James is clear that we can be healed if we pray in faith.'

'Aah! You mean the passage in chapter 5?'

'Yes. I can't see that it means anything other than what Tom tells me it means. And, as he said, we're not to be guided by the opinions of other people or the fear of failure—even other people's failures—when they've invoked this promise. He says: "if the conditions are fulfilled—if the elders pray for the sick with the prayer of faith—then the sick will be healed."'

'Are you sure it only says "healed"?' Jim asked, as he stretched out for his Bible. 'After all, if it does state "shall be healed", it leaves no room for excusing God not fulfilling the promise.' He quickly flicked through the pages and found the passage Dave had cited.

'I can see what you mean; it does say "healed"! Perhaps I'd better check this out. Will you excuse me a moment?'

Jim got up and left the room. Within a minute or so he returned with several Bibles.

'These translations might help unravel the mystery.' He handed Dave two of them, and asked him to find the passage while he looked it up in the others.

Dave started: 'The *Authorised* says: "and the prayer of faith shall save the sick, and the Lord shall raise him up".' Jim responded: 'Well, the *New English Bible* says: "and the prayer offered in faith will save the sick man, the Lord will raise him from his bed".'

They picked up the other bibles and, within seconds, were comparing translations again.

'*The Good News Bible* says: "This prayer made in faith will heal the sick person; the Lord will restore him to health".' Dave chipped in, 'and *The Amplified Bible* says, "and the prayer (that is) of faith will save him that is sick and the Lord will restore him." '

'What's it saying?' asked Dave, mystified by the various renderings.

By this time, his pastor was flicking through the pages of a Greek New Testament. He soon found the passage. He smiled and looked up at Dave.

'It says the Lord will "save"! It's the word *so¯sei.'*

'Then why so many different translations?'

'It's because the word actually contains all those different ideas. It's like the passage in Timothy,[11] where Paul says God is the Saviour of all men, especially those who believe. The noun *so¯te¯r* is linked to the same word used here in James. Paul is not saying God saves all people from their sins especially those who believe, but that He saves all people who call upon Him in different ways, and He especially saves—truly and completely saves—those who believe on the Lord Jesus.'

'Can you explain that further?'

'Take, for example, the Philippian jailer's question: "What must I do to be saved?" He wasn't thinking of spiritual salvation or forgiveness of sins. He was worried about losing his life! He feared the consequences of being responsible for the chaos in the jail! Failure to keep the prisoners secure was life-threatening. That immediate danger could be met by turning to God. Once he'd done this, Paul went on to tell him the good news of Jesus; and then he believed at the spiritual level.'[12]

'I see, so when people are in danger and ask God for protection, they're asking for salvation.'

'Yes, in a limited way, but not in the most important way.'

'How does this affect James 5?'

'Well, it seems to me James is saying that when people are sick, God is going to "save" them through the prayers of the elders. Yes, sometimes that might mean healing, but remember that God might choose instead to comfort and sustain them in their illness. The one thing that's sure is that He *will* act in some way on their behalf.'

'It seems to make some sense.'

'Yes, I think so, too. Just look at the context of the passage. Earlier, James cited Job and the prophets[13] as men of faith. Even though Job wasn't immediately delivered from his distress, he was sustained through it. In fact, if you look back a few verses, James stresses that God's promises are going to be completely fulfilled at the coming of Jesus.[14] Although God will often graciously answers our prayers for the sick, the fact remains that we cannot know complete freedom from trouble or sickness until then!'

'You know, Jim, I think you're probably right. But how does it work out in practice?'

'Let me try to relate this to a situation I've known. Do you remember Margaret Rayner, Ben's auntie, who died last year?'

'Yes, she was a lovely woman.'

Jim nodded. 'I remember going to pray for her with the elders. She expected to be healed and spoke positively of how much better she felt after we'd been. But her next visit to the clinic brought very bad news. We continued to go and pray with her, and she told me something I'll never forget. She said that, in some strange way, the love and prayers of Christians who came to pray with her lifted her out of the distress she was in and helped her cope. She was always glad to have us visit—not just once, but regularly. Through our prayers and care, the Lord was extending His loving hand and she was experiencing His *salvation*.'

'And one day,' Dave said, 'she, with all believers, will know God's salvation in its fullness, including being made like the Lord Jesus. You know, Jim,' he continued, 'Margaret was an incredible example of a Christian facing suffering. I always marvelled at her.'

'She was! I felt very humbled every time I went to see her. I've little doubt that the Lord was supremely honoured in her testimony, possibly in a way she never appreciated. She experienced His salvation in relation to her physical and spiritual needs.'

'Come to think of it, isn't there a similarity between the problems Christians face who hold to a belief that *everyone* should be healed and the problems the Thessalonian Christians faced?'

'How do you mean?' asked Jim.

'Well, they were deeply hurt because Christian relatives and friends had died. They had to learn that even death had been sanctified and become part of God's purpose and that they'd not missed God's best because of bereavement.'[15]

'I'm sure you're right, Dave!'

'Let me just go over what you've said. You say that there are clear examples of even the apostles and their helpers not being healed; that mass healing is often something which accompanies the outpouring of God's Spirit; that the only time Christians are promised they'll be entirely delivered from all physical sickness is at Christ's return, and that "healed" and "saved" are translations of the same Greek word in which there are many shades of deliverance.'

'Well done!' smiled Jim, in amazement that Dave had been able to recall the essential points of the discussion so clearly.

'Goodness,' said Dave, looking at the clock above the fireplace, 'I hadn't realised the time!'

'Neither had I … I'll be in trouble! Jo left me strict instructions before she went out with the girls. I had to make sure I made you a hot drink. Can you spare the time for one now?'

'I'm sorry,' laughed Dave, 'it's very kind, but I promised Becky I'd be back by 9.30. Thanks for tonight, Jim; you've helped so much. Perhaps some other time we could talk through another problem?'

Questions to Ponder

1. Is it 'unspiritual' to test people's claims concerning answers to prayer?
2. Does all scripture say that prayer will be answered in the way the prayer thinks it should?
3. What evidence is there in the NT that not all sick Christian people are healed?
4. What was the experience of the apostles regarding the miraculous?
5. Does James 5:14–15 say all will be healed? What are the possible meanings of this crucial verse?
6. In what way(s) is God a Saviour? Is it permissible to invite unbelievers to ask for God's help?

The Right Path

Prayer and Guidance

Jim pulled up under the street light that was outside Dave and Becky's house. A curtain was pulled back, and Dave waved to say they were on their way. Within a few minutes, Jim was out of his car and standing in cold March rain to welcome his two young friends. He opened the back door after taking their case and, while Becky settled herself into the back seat, the luggage was put into the boot.

'Good,' said Jim, as he and Dave slammed their front doors closed. 'I'm glad you were able to get time off at such short notice. Your boss didn't mind?'

'No, he was really good. When I told him how bad Dad was and that we'd been offered a lift, he was keen for me to go. It's just great you're going to Newcastle tonight. We really do appreciate this, Jim. Being so far away from our families at times like this is very difficult.'

'I know. When we were first married we found it a problem to keep in touch as well—Jo's family was up in the north-east, mine was in Liverpool, and we were down in Hertfordshire! I dare say you also find the pressure of affording unexpected journeys as real as we did, especially when you haven't got a car!'

'That's right!' said Becky. 'When we heard Dave's dad was ill, we felt awful because we couldn't see how we could get up North to see him straightaway. We thought we'd try to get a car before the baby's born—we just didn't get it soon enough.'

Soon they'd reached the slip road coming onto the motorway. The rain had eased and the traffic was light, so it was only a matter of seconds before Jim had reached the cruising speed he wanted.

'I thought I'd attempt three jobs at once,' he said.

'What do you mean?'

'Well, I thought that, in going to the conference, I could give you a lift to Durham and we could continue our discussion on prayer on the way!'

'That's great!' responded Dave. 'Becky and I looked very carefully at those passages you mentioned last time and found they sorted our thinking out quite a lot. Did you have a subject in mind?'

'Not especially, though I did wonder if you'd like to talk about prayer and guidance.'

Becky enthused: 'I'd love to be in on that one! I get so confused about it. There've been times when I've felt very sure about something and prayed, yet it just didn't work out as I expected.'

'That's a good phrase to begin with, Becky.'

'What is?'

'"As I expected!" That's often the problem with guidance—we think our expectations are in line with God's will. When they get out of control, we get confused if not hurt. I remember a boy back in Liverpool,' laughed Jim, 'he was very keen on a girl in the youth group called Olive. He prayed for her; and when he read in the Psalms[16] that his children would be like olives, he felt that God was giving him a promise that he'd marry her and have a family!'

'Did he?'

'No! They're both happily married now, but not to each other!'

'Well, do you remember Steve at uni, Dave? He once said that the Lord had told him he was going to marry me. You know, he never got over the fact you came on the scene.'

'But, Jim, should we expect guidance to be a hit-and-miss affair? I never made any claim that I was guided to go out with Becky. I just loved her qualities and her company. It seemed the inevitable next step to allow our friendship to develop.'

'And the evidence that it really was of God is seen in a couple who obviously love each other!'

'So how do you understand guidance?'

'Well, Becky, I see it as the outworking of God's purpose in the daily grind. Sometimes it involves the spectacular, but not very often.'

'Can you explain?' Dave chipped in.

'OK. Did you feel guided to accept this lift?'

'No.'

'Nor did I feel guided to ask you! You knew from your knowledge of God's will that ignoring the needs of your Dad and Mum would have gone against it, and, if I was to rationalise my response to knowing your need, I didn't need guidance to tell me what God would have me do. Helping you out with a lift was the only right thing. I would have needed "special" guidance not to have approached you.'

'Hey', said Dave. 'That's the reverse of what Tom would say. But it does fit in.'

'That's right. Remember Paul's vision to enter Macedonia? It'd been preceded by a very strong sense of the Spirit's guidance not to do what seemed the next obvious step.[17] In other words, sanctified common sense is the norm, unless there's a strong sense of God's intervention.'

'Have you got any examples of sanctified common sense?' asked Becky.

'Well, the whole missionary strategy of Paul was based on a common-sense plan. His strategy was to go to the great centres of the ancient world in the hope that he could establish churches there and that the new Christians, who would remain in those cities, would go on to evangelise their own people.'[18]

'But you're not saying that God doesn't give some sort of revelation beyond sanctified common sense, are you?'

'Of course not! An obvious example is Philip, leaving the fantastic happenings in Samaria to go into the desert to meet the Ethiopian eunuch![19] But if you read Acts honestly, you'll see there are no claims that regular daily guidance like this was the norm.'

'How do you feel about people who constantly say that the Lord has told them to do things?'

'I'd have to say, Dave, they have quite a different experience from the New Testament believers!'

'But you don't deny that the Lord does lead?'

'No,' laughed Jim, obviously aware of the concern in Becky's voice. 'But I believe He wants us to accept that there're lots of incidents we must take responsibility for. Even Paul backed off from attributing everything to direct guidance.'[20]

'I see,' said Dave. 'Claiming something to be God's will can become an irresponsible cliché that backfires.'

'That's right! If we use that expression lightly, we'll finish up hurt. I know lots of Christians who've told me what God has told them what He's going to do with them or give them. To this day they haven't come to terms with the fact that things haven't worked out as they believed they would.'

'Such as?'

'Well, a couple in our first church told me the Lord had said He'd give them a healthy baby when they were expecting their first child. They were devastated when their little girl was born with a serious abnormality.'

'Was the promise fulfilled in a later child?' asked Becky.

'Tragically, no,' responded Jim. 'Steve was killed in an accident at work, leaving his wife to bring little Hannah up on her own.'

The journey was flying by, with the three absorbed in conversation. When Jim asked if they'd like a break at the next service station, Becky thought it was a good idea. She'd been a little uncomfortable sitting in one position for a long time, and it was at times like this that she knew she was 5 months pregnant!. Soon Jim was indicating he was pulling off the motorway and, before long, they were huddled around a table with large mugs of coffee.

'Do you have any views on praying for miracles?' asked Dave.

'Not particularly, though I find myself surprised at the many claims that are plainly not of the Lord.'

'Is it right to pray for them?'

'It would be wrong to say that we must never pray for miracles, but I think there's an unhealthy interest in the "unusual" today that isn't a reflection of New Testament Christianity.'

'How do you mean, Jim?'

'Well, I think the early believers knew God could work miracles, but they didn't normally ask for them. They saw miracles further down the list of priorities than is common in some circles today.'

'What was at the top of their list, in your opinion?'

'Well, prayer always concentrated on two things: the quality of life believers lived and the advancement of the gospel.[21] Both were vital for the Lord's glory.'

'But didn't they pray for a miraculous deliverance for Peter from prison?'

'Did they, Dave?' responded Jim, with a smile.

'Well, that's what it seemed when they had their prayer meeting in Rhoda's home.'[22]

'Then why didn't they believe it was Peter who was outside?' asked Jim.

'Because they'd lacked faith in their praying,' was the immediate reply.

'Now that I find interesting! God only answers prayer if prayed in faith. Their prayer was answered, but it wasn't in faith.'

Dave screwed his face up as he thought. 'That's a difficult one,' he said.

'Not if you stop insisting they were praying for his deliverance,' suggested Jim. 'If they were praying for strength and faith for Peter, then it's reasonable they should be amazed at his deliverance!'

'So you're saying the disciples never prayed for Peter's deliverance, only for his faith to be sustained. Come to think of it, that makes sense. After all, some of their leaders had already been brutally murdered—John the Baptist,[23] the Lord himself,[24] and Stephen.[25] If they had sealed the truth with their lives, did the disciples have a right to demand that God should stop Peter's death?'

'Absolutely,' said Jim. 'The New Testament's full of promises that Christ's followers would suffer for Him[26] and that they'd be sustained. As I said before, most of the praying in the Bible is to do with asking God for His sustaining grace and for power to witness.'

'But you're not saying that God doesn't perform miracles, are you?'

'No, Becky, He certainly does; but the most important miracles are the redemption of His people and their daily experience of the benefits of His salvation, making them more like Christ.'

Before long, the three friends had returned to the car, and the final leg of their journey got underway.

'Jim, you've given us lots to think about tonight. Could you list the steps you see involved in guidance?'

'Certainly! I'd say there were two types of guidance: daily and crucial. For daily guidance, I think there're two important steps. The first one is that, as I learn God's will from the Scriptures, I try to put it into practice. It's only as I live according to God's will that His will is going to be worked out in my life. Secondly, I've discovered that I have to commit my day to God,[27] asking Him to order the events of the day and bless my involvement in them.'

'So, daily guidance is understanding God's Word and living by it?'

'That's right, Becky!' responded Jim. 'I spoke to a young woman once who constantly spoke of the ways God guided her. At the same time, she was in a relationship with a married man. The Bible is absolutely clear she was not being guided by God but walking in darkness.'

'You mentioned guidance in crucial matters. What do you mean by this?' asked Dave.

'Oh, these are the big decisions in life: marriage; career choice; a sense of call to leave employment to become more available for Christian service; and so on.'

'How do you deal with these?'

'Well, first of all I ask if there's anything in conflict with God's revealed will. For example, marriage to a non-Christian would be ruled out by God's Word;[28] employment in an industry that exploited people's weaknesses would be another instance. It would be ridiculous to claim to be guided by God if I was doing something that was not His will.'

'Having checked that out, what's the next step?'

'If confronted with alternatives, I'd ask which choice would most glorify the Lord. Take Pete Fielder, for example. Remember he was offered a job in London? It had a massive salary and great prospects. He turned it down because, when he went into it carefully, he realised he'd hardly see his family and it would cut right across opportunities to use his gifts for the Lord. He could see his spare time would be almost non-existent.'[29]

'That's a hard one,' responded Dave. 'It must be very difficult to keep an eye on priorities when you're offered so much money.'

'It is! Sadly all too many Christians automatically measure God's blessing by the yardstick of prosperity and promotion. These may well be blessings, but in themselves they're just not evidence of true discipleship.'

'Is it wrong to choose what we want to do?' enquired Becky.

'No, God's will for us isn't destructive; He uses our natural abilities. In fact, if I'm in a job I hate doing, I'd have to question my spiritual state or my suitability. Having said that, a test of real discipleship is to be prepared to do whatever brings glory to God.'

'Is there another principle for discovering God's will?'

'Yes, Dave, listen to the advice of Christian friends and family—people who really know you! I don't mean people who flatter and don't tell the truth, but people who really care—are spiritually minded and know your weaknesses as well as your strengths.'[30]

'Don't you think you should have mentioned prayer—I mean, shouldn't that be first?'

'It's not only first, it's first, last and all the time![31] But it's not a magic method for getting the right answer.'

'What do you mean?' queried Becky.

'I mean that the whole of our lives are to be lived in dependence on God and obedience to Him. If we're not consistently seeking to follow Him, committing our ways to Him and serving Him, then prayer doesn't suddenly release the genie out of the bottle, telling us what to do.'

The rain returned with a vengeance and, as the spray of passing cars and lorries reduced visibility, Jim found it difficult to answer Dave and Becky's questions with the care they deserved. And so, as they neared Durham, the conversation on prayer came to a close.

'We turn off here,' said Dave, as the car approached a slip road. 'Mam and Dad live only a few miles from the junction.'

Before long, Dave was guiding Jim through the streets of Durham to the terrace of houses where he'd been bought up.

'My,' he said, 'it's good to be home!'

Questions to Ponder

1. What is the norm for guidance?
2. How were the apostles guided?
3. What was the attitude of the early church to miracles?
4. What was the focus of the prayers for the NT believers?
5. Is it possible to experience God's guidance while rejecting what his word teaches?
6. What advice does Jim give over guidance in 'crucial matters'?

No Good if Detached

Prayer and God's Promises

It was Sunday morning in early April, and Jim was standing at Emmanuel's church door, waiting for members of his congregation to leave. The trickle of people had dried up, and he was about to go back into the lounge, where the majority were still chatting over coffee. He was reflecting on the sermon he'd just preached—he wished he'd expressed himself more clearly and persuasively. He felt he'd failed miserably to convey the wonder of the theme he'd just preached on.

'Are you coming in, Jim?' a voice enquired from behind, breaking into his thoughts. 'It's quite cold out here. I think you'll wait a long time before anyone else leaves.'

It was Simon, one of his elders. He'd brought a cup of coffee out to him.

'Thanks, Simon. I could just do with that. It felt dry in there this morning. Has someone altered the thermostat setting?'

'I'll check it out. It was warm in there!'

Jim wandered through to the lounge, acknowledging different folk and chatting with those he knew had problems. Just as he finished a conversation with an elderly lady, he caught sight of Dave walking towards him with a friend. He hadn't seen this young man before. He was probably a Christian as he'd sung the hymns in the service with such enthusiasm.

'Hello, Dave,' Jim said, stretching out his hand. 'How are you, and how's Becky?'

'She's fine thanks, but very tired! She didn't sleep too well last night and just didn't cope with getting ready in time, I'm afraid!'

Realising that the conversation had not included Dave's friend, Jim turned to him. 'Hello,' he said, stretching out his hand. 'It's nice to meet you.'

'Oh, I'm sorry, Jim. It was rude of me not to introduce you. This is Tom, my friend from work.'

The name rang an immediate bell with Jim, and his mind went back to that freezing January night when Tom was first mentioned.

'Thanks for the message this morning,' Tom said. 'I must say you highlighted things I'd never thought of before. I found it really exciting to see how God gives different people insights into His Word, and then gifts them to share it effectively.'

Jim smiled in recognition of Tom's encouragement. He was somewhat surprised at his genuine warmth and open-mindedness. Somehow, he had an image of a forceful young man who was out to put all 'lesser' believers right. This was far from the truth. He clearly had a love for his Saviour, and just as touching was his obvious love for other Christians.

'Tom works with me,' said Dave. 'He's one of our brightest engineers. He grasps everything first time from systems controls right through to filling in requisites for pencils!'

'He's very kind,' Tom interrupted, 'but there are many instances when Dave is way ahead of me, and if I do learn quickly it's because he's a great teacher!'

'But surely you don't teach in your job?' Jim said, with a puzzled look at Dave.

'Not exactly teach,' interjected Tom, 'but he is supervising me while I get eased into my new post—and I couldn't have a better supervisor! But talking about teaching, there was one thing this morning that left me wondering what you had in mind. You said God's promises are not to be taken at their immediate face value but are to be seen in their contexts. I'd like to hear more about that.'

Jim smiled at Dave with a smile that said: 'It looks as though we got to this one quicker than expected!'

'Are you in a hurry?' he asked Tom.

'No. Our service normally goes on a lot longer than it did this morning, in any case, I'm going to Dave and Becky's for lunch.'

Jim suggested that they grabbed coffees and sat down at one of the tables.

'I can understand why you want some clarification on that statement. If it's not seen in its correct context, it can convey something quite different from what I intended.'

Tom's keen eyes flashed as he saw how easily misunderstanding can be unintentionally introduced.

'I think I get you,' he said. 'You're not actually saying don't *ever* take God's promises at their face value but only take them at face value when you're sure you know what they really mean.'

Jim turned to Dave and said, 'I see what you mean about quick understanding. Do you know, Tom,' he continued, 'I took over half an hour to explain that to someone once.'

Tom laughed.

'Can you help me to apply that principle? It's obviously true, but where and how does it need to be applied?'

'Dave and I've been talking things over about prayer in the last few months. This is one of the areas I was going to cover with him.'

'Great!' said Tom, with obvious excitement. 'Tell me more!'

Jim looked at Dave, and it was obvious he was happy to stay a little longer. Jim began slowly, trying to think through how he was going to express himself.

'If we're not careful to keep a particular promise in the setting in which it was given,' he said, 'we are more than likely to get hurt with disappointment.'

Jim continued in his hesitancy, watching carefully for responses from the two men to judge if they were following his thoughts.

'All too often, I've believed I known what should be done in a given situation and have told God what He ought to do. I've quoted a promise to show that He was obliged to do it—a promise like, "If you ask anything in my name, I will do it"[32]—and then considered I'd prayed in faith, not realising I'd tempted God and that my prayer was exactly the opposite of one in the Spirit.'

Dave couldn't conceive of Jim ever doing such a thing. He'd come to respect his judgement in many areas, especially in spiritual matters. He couldn't help asking, 'How do you mean?'

'Do you remember the temptation when Jesus was challenged to throw Himself off the pinnacle of the Temple?[33] Satan quoted verses from Psalm 91, which said that God would give His angels charge in case He hit His foot against a rock. Satan was using Scripture to put pressure on Jesus to do something that was the very opposite of God's will.'

'I've fallen to that sort of pressure in the past,' Jim continued, 'and been deeply hurt when (not literally, mind you!) I was smashed against the rocks. I became angry with God that He'd not kept His side of the bargain when I'd stepped out in faith and kept mine. Have either of you ever felt like that?'

Dave nodded, but Tom was staring hard at Jim across the table. His eyes then dropped and he looked at his hands clasped in front of him. He was obviously trying to cope with his thoughts. 'Don't you', he stumbled, 'don't you think God could have been teaching you a lesson?'

'Yes, but I suppose everything can teach us lessons if we're willing to learn. And, in that sense, yes, God redeems our foolishness. But I see no evidence in Scripture that He ever sends His children up blind alleys to teach them lessons.'

Tom continued to look as though he was having difficulty with what Jim was saying.

'To be honest,' he said slowly, 'there have been times when I've wondered why God didn't do exactly as I expected; but doesn't God answer by saying "no" sometimes?'

'That's true,' said Jim, 'but if he says no then it is clear that he had never actually promised to say "yes". He isn't a God who keeps changing His mind! If we find what we expected has not happened after having claimed that God had said it would happen in response to our prayers, we must accept that we were wrong, not God. We must accept that we got caught up with enthusiasm and we mistakenly took it to be the Spirit confirming the Word.'

Dave had been listening carefully and felt he wanted to query Jim on a matter.

'Don't you think there are prayers we might never see answered? You're not wanting to say that all prayers not obviously answered spring from such enthusiasm, are you?'

'No, I don't want to suggest that. Prayers for the conversion of people, for example, may be answered after we've died—we might never see the answer on this side of eternity. What I'm concerned about is the sort of praying that demands immediate answers and holds God to account simply by unthinkingly quoting Scriptures to Him.'

'I know what you mean,' confessed Tom. He turned to Dave. 'Do you remember me telling you about that meeting with the Australian evangelist a few weeks ago? One of my friends prayed that the hall would be full and we all responded by claiming the passage in Matthew 18, where it says: "If two or three of you are agreed on earth it shall be done."[34] We were certain it was going to be a huge success because we'd prayed in faith. When the night came, it poured down! Only about fifty turned up and they were all Christians! What I can't understand is why the Lord didn't honour His promise. He did say if two or three agreed, He would do it.'

'I think we need to look at that Scripture carefully,' said Jim, flicking over the pages of his Bible to Matthew 18. 'Look,' he said, turning it round so that Tom could see. 'That's the verse you held on to, wasn't it?' He had his finger on verse 19.

'That's it!' said Tom.

'Now, tell me, what are the verses immediately in front of it talking about?'

Tom's eyes scanned the page. 'It's about correction and church discipline,' he replied.

'Exactly! So what do you think this promise is about?'

Dave couldn't wait for Tom to ponder the obvious answer and assess its significance for his view of prayer. He jumped in with the excitement of seeing something he hadn't seen before.

'It's about church discipline,' he said. 'It's a promise for the church when it's seeking Christ's help in matters of discipline.'

Jim nodded, and, within a few seconds, Tom raised his eyes to meet Jim's and said, 'We unwittingly did the very thing Satan tried to do with Jesus, didn't we? We argued what God ought to do and then tried to persuade Him to do it by misusing Scripture.'

'No, there's a big difference, I think,' Jim smiled, sympathetically. 'You and I have sometimes asked amiss[35] whilst earnestly and honestly seeking God's glory; Satan didn't do that. Satan was deceptive, whereas we were simply mistaken.'

'Phew!' said a relieved Tom, and the three men laughed. 'You had me really worried there! Are there any other passages we tend to misuse?'

'Well, another that comes to mind is in Mark 11. It's the passage where Jesus said "if you have faith you will say to this mountain, be plucked up and cast into the sea, and it will happen."'[36]

'How can it mean anything else?' Dave asked.

'Oh, it means exactly what it says, God is able to do amazing things; but let's have a look again at its setting.' Jim thumbed through the pages of his Bible once again.

'Have a look!' he said, pushing the Bible over the table so that it was between the two young engineers.

They spent several minutes reading and turning back to the previous page.

'It seems Jesus had cursed a fig tree the day before, and the disciples were amazed when the next day it had withered up.[37] In response to their amazement, He said they could do greater things even with a little faith—things like casting a mountain into the sea.'

'Fine,' said Jim; 'but that's only one piece of the jigsaw, Tom. If we're really to understand the statement, we need to connect it to the other pieces.'

'What are they?' Tom's mind was trying to think what the missing pieces could possibly be.

'Well,' said Jim, looking at him, 'you've told us the preceding setting: the day before, Jesus cursed the fig tree. What did He do after that?'

'He went to Jerusalem and, after entering the Temple, He threw over the tables of the money changers,' Dave replied.

'Yes, and what was special about His entrance into Jerusalem?'

'He was declaring Himself to be the Messiah,' Tom snapped, excited at the picture he could see building up in his imagination.

'Fine,' said Jim. 'So here's the picture. Jesus, going up to Jerusalem, saw a fig tree. It was not, in fact, the time for fruit—the fig tree produces leaves before its fruit. Jesus examined it to see if it had any fruit to satisfy Him. It's a theme we often get in the Old Testament of

God looking for fruitfulness from the Jewish people—not prosperity of course, but righteousness.'

'I see,' said Tom. 'So Jesus's cursing of the fig tree was not an act of temper—it had a symbolic significance!'

'And that links up with what He did in a prophetic act near to the Temple,' contributed Dave. 'He was acting out symbolically the judgement that would soon come on the corrupt nerve centre of the nation's life!'

'So, how does the Messianic entry into Jerusalem fit in?' asked Jim, excited to see if his two students were going in the right direction.

'He was not only entering symbolically as the Messiah of peace but also the Messiah who would purify,' Tom said, beating Dave by a fraction of a second.

'But how does moving the mountain by prayer fit in?' Dave enquired.

'For that we have to go back to the book of Zechariah.' And, flicking through his Bible, Jim found chapter 14. Before sliding it back across the table, he paused and said, 'What we must appreciate is that chapters 9–14 of Zechariah were very important to the early Christians. Many would have learnt them by heart because they explained in a nutshell what God had said He'd do through his Servant, the Messiah. In fact, it's in this section that the predictions about Jesus's entry into Jerusalem;[38] of His being crucified;[39] the

Shepherd being smitten;[40] and the payment of thirty pieces of silver[41] to Judas are made.'

'Wow,' said Tom, 'you can see why the early church saw those chapters as important!'

'But there's a prophecy about the Messiah in the section that isn't fulfilled. Look! Jim slid the Bible between the two men with his finger on 14:4.

Dave began to read it aloud: 'On that day, His feet will stand on the Mount of Olives, east of Jerusalem, and the Mount of Olives will be split in two from east to west, forming a great valley, with half of the mountain moving north and half moving south.'

Jim spoke after he'd allowed them time to think over its significance. 'You two engineers will be interested in something I read in the *New Scientist Magazine* many years ago,' he said. 'An article actually referred to this passage when a construction company had been forced to abandon building a hotel on the Mount of Olives. A geological report showed there was a major flaw running through it, and it only needed an earthquake for it to split in two.'

'That's amazing!' said Tom. 'And doesn't it say in the New Testament that Jesus left us from the Mount of Olives?'[42]

Jim nodded in agreement. 'Yes, that's absolutely right.'

Dave's mind was already gathering the pieces together. They were beginning to give him the completed picture.

'I think I see now,' he said. 'When Jesus said: "You shall say to this mountain", it was not any old mountain. What He was saying is, "You, by faith, can be instrumental in bringing about the most momentous event in history, the return of Jesus Christ."'

'Exactly!' said Jim, 'and, of course, the mountain that they could see as they approached Jerusalem from Jericho was ...'

'The Mount of Olives,' they both said in unison.

Jim looked at his watch. 'Goodness, I'll get shot. Look at the time!'

They'd been so engrossed in the discussion that they hadn't realised they were the only ones left in the building.

'We really must go too,' said Dave. 'But, thanks, Jim. I can see how this links up with what you said about the promise in James 5 being kept in context. I'll try and explain that one to Tom over beef and roast potatoes.'

'Marvellous!' said Tom, 'sounds like a great lunch!'

Questions to Ponder

1. How should the promises of Scripture be used in prayer, and what should control the way they are appropriated?
2. What is the difference between mistaken use of Scripture and the way Satan uses Scripture?
3. Why did Jesus curse the fig tree?

4. What is the significance of the Mount of Olives for future prophecy and why is it important?

Prayer is not a Joke

Prayer and Evangelism

'Hi, Jim! I didn't expect to see you today,' beamed Dave.

'I'm sorry, Dave, I did say I couldn't make it; but when I saw the sun I decided that writing on May Bank Holiday wasn't a good idea after all. I'll probably regret it next week when I'm due to finish the article! Still, I couldn't resist coming—to think that Jo and the girls would be out while I was stuck indoors wasn't my idea of a perfect bank holiday.'

'You missed last year's hike, didn't you?'

'I did, I had that wretched chest infection. Goodness, it doesn't seem a year since then!'

'Are Jo and the girls coming? I can't see them anywhere.'

'They'll be along soon', replied Jim. 'Jo needed to make some arrangements, so I left her with the girls—and they'll grab any extra time that's on offer to get ready! She had a few calls to make, so they won't be long.'

It was a perfect, bright and sunny day for the church's annual hike, and Dave had been carefully planning the route for weeks. He'd decided that the group would travel to Baslow, in the Peak District, by car, and from there to do an easy five mile walk before driving back to the church in Chesterfield in time for tea.

'Has anyone seen Ben?' Dave shouted. 'He's got the maps—we can't go without him.'

'Yes, I'm here,' shouted someone from the back of the crowd. Dave looked over and saw Ben's arm waving above the heads of the party. He had copies of the map in his hand, which he'd printed off for the drivers in case they got separated from the convoy.

'Can you pass them round, Ben? We'll hang on for another five minutes and then we really must go.'

'But Liz said that she'd be late,' shouted one of the young people. 'Her mum forgot to wake her and she was still in her dressing-gown five minutes ago.'

Dave groaned, but the group was full of excitement and nobody minded. Children were racing around, dodging between the chatting adults; dogs were straining at their leashes to be on the move and drivers were pouring over maps to make sure they knew the route.

Just as Dave was anxiously looking at his watch, Jo came round the corner with Sophie, Emma and Liz. When the young people saw a very dishevelled Liz, a cry of 'Oh no—we thought we'd managed to leave you behind!' came from one of her best friends.

Soon the cars were loaded and, just as the parish clock chimed ten, the first of them pulled away for the half-hour journey to the starting point of the hike.

The countryside was beautiful! The fresh spring air made the colours of emerging flowers look vivid—even the burnished gold of the buttercups looked wonderful. While it was definitely a day for sweaters and anoraks, the blue sky was cloudless. Soon the party was assembled at its starting point and was quickly out of the car park and through the village onto the bridle path.

'You look lost', said Jo, as she and Jim drew alongside Dave. 'Is Becky staying at home?'

'Yes, she thought it might send her blood pressure up if she came, so she's giving a lick of paint to an old family crib we were loaned. It was my Auntie Doreen's—all the babies in the family have had their turn in it! Jim …' he said, turning to look at his pastor, 'you know you said you'd talk about prayer and salvation sometime? If you could spare some time today, I'd be really grateful—but I don't want to stop you mixing with other people.'

'That's OK! I've had a chat with most folk already.'

'Well, I've been wondering about your sermon a few weeks ago on John 17, where Jesus said He wasn't praying for the world but for those who were given Him out of the world.[43] Is it wrong to pray for non-Christians?'

'Phew ...' responded Jim. 'You certainly pick them, don't you?'

'I don't intend to,' laughed Dave. 'It's just that it seems important to know if prayer should be directed at unsaved friends or not. I wouldn't have thought it shouldn't,' he continued, 'but in the light of what Jesus said, it has made me wonder.'

'It's made me wonder a lot over the years, too,' confessed Jim. 'It's a problem that anyone who thinks seriously about prayer has to face at some point, but it isn't easy to give a definitive answer. The problem is that if it isn't tackled, it leaves the whole topic of prayer open to misunderstanding and, perhaps, false expectations, which can cause serious problems.'

'I've noticed that you always pray for non-Christians,' Dave commented.

'That's right, but perhaps you've noticed how I pray for them.'

'Yes—I've noticed you're guarded in what you ask. I assume you hold back from claiming that salvation will come to for everyone because you believe in God's sovereignty.'

'That's right,' Jim said, as he unearthed a rather dusty old packet of sweets from the depths of his anorak pocket and offered them to Jo and Dave. 'I find this to be the most difficult area to know how to pray in, yet the least difficult to actually pray.'

'That sounds Irish,' Dave said, smiling.

'Sounds double-Dutch to me,' quipped Jo, who'd been walking alongside the men and following their conversation.

'It's the result of being caught in the paradox of man's responsibility and God's sovereignty. I find it easy to pray for God to save people because I'm confronted with the simple scriptural truth that men outside of Christ are under an eternal sentence of separation from God, despite his willingness to save.[44] To know people *can* be saved if only they would repent and believe causes such an inner cry that it's virtually impossible not to pray for them.'

'But then you're faced with the same problem I raised when I first came to see you,' said Dave. 'If God is sovereign, what's the point in praying?'

'That's right—and do you remember what we found in the Scriptures?'

'Yes, I do,' Dave replied, 'We've got to keep all truth in perspective. One truth on its own gets distorted and becomes quite different from what it means in its scriptural setting. I must say, although I've been making massive efforts to keep this in mind, it is difficult to keep the balance.'

'That doesn't surprise me,' smiled Jim. 'I've never met anyone who finds it easy. It's keeping two totally different perspectives in focus at the same time. But as you're asking about prayer and salvation, I'm going to bring in another perspective. We often see ourselves like medical orderlies on a battle field, caught up with caring for the wounded. It'd be disastrous if they persuaded their General to focus on the soldiers' safety rather than on his costly strategy of conquering the enemy. He'd have information about the enemy they would have no idea about. He'd have war objectives that would affect his decisions and he'd expect them to obey his commands so they could be achieved. He'd not expect them to argue, that's for sure!'

'I see,' said Dave. 'You're suggesting we keep our eyes on the Lord and His ultimate goal rather than on our own wishes, however laudable?'

'You've got it!'

'How do you find this affects your praying?' enquired Dave.

'Well,' Jim began carefully, 'at one time, when my emphasis was for individuals to be saved, it was relatively rare that prayers were answered. I could give examples when they were—but there were plenty of "failures". Then I realised that if I got prayer answered even one in four times, it actually proved nothing. You know, the whole attraction of gambling is that the punter keeps getting it right at fairly regular intervals. Claims that my prayers would be answered were no more than what statistically I ought to have scored, considering the number of requests I was making.'

Dave nodded in obvious agreement.

'Then I looked carefully at what the Scriptures were saying,' continued Jim. 'I didn't want to read anything into them because that meant I'd only see my own desires and understanding. When we read the Bible, the big danger is we're like little children looking into a pond: we think we're looking at something in the water, but, in reality, we're only looking at our reflection! When I tried hard not to read my own prejudices into the Bible, I began to see that the Scriptures were saying something different from what I'd always understood. They were dealing with issues that were much bigger than my thinking. They were dealing with communities, even with nations, turning to the Lord.'

'Do you mean to say we shouldn't pray for individuals to be saved?' queried Jo, who once again broke her silence.

'No, not at all! But praying for just anyone who comes to mind isn't the pattern I find in Scripture. Praying for people the Spirit moves us to pray for, and burdens us with, is a different matter. What we really need is God's burden for the unconverted.'

'Do you think it's possible we don't experience the Spirit prompting us like this is because we haven't got the bigger perspective?'

'That's certainly my experience, Dave,' admitted Jim.

'But, Jim,' said Jo, feeling confused and threatened, 'you seem to be saying: "don't pray for individual conversions".'

'I'm sorry if it comes across that way—I don't intend to mean that. But I think our praying should be about God's glory and the accomplishment of His purposes, which includes the salvation of sinners. If we miss the fact that salvation is part of the theme of the glory of God and concentrate on the necessity of conversion in isolation from its proper context, then we can finish up justifying almost any method that wins people. The conversion of the lost is not an end in itself; its end is God's glory. If in seeking to win the lost we do things that dishonour God, then we have gone terribly wrong in our thinking.'

'What Scriptures do you base this on, other than John 17, of course?' asked Dave.

'It's not so much which Scriptures I base it on, Dave, it's the whole flow of Scripture—both Old and New Testaments. Before coming to this view, I lacked scriptural support. I came to realise, for example, that there're no prayer requests from the apostles for the conversion of individuals in any of their letters, nor are there any examples of the type of praying for the unsaved that we're caught up with today.'

'Then what did the New Testament church pray about?' asked Dave.

'Always the glory of God and the need for Him to empower their witness! Because the early Christians had this perspective, they weren't despondent about their circumstances[45] or even their apparent lack of success. How people responded to the gospel was God's responsibility; their responsibility was to make it known clearly, so all could hear of the grace of God in His Son. They were so captivated by this grace that the chief purpose of their lives was to magnify God—and that meant that they had to proclaim Jesus to unbelievers and, very often, suffer rejection as a result.'

Their concentration was suddenly broken by one of the children crying behind them. Dave turned to see Molly's mum Sarah picking her up and hastily moving as quickly as she could to catch up with the stragglers of the party. Behind Sarah and Molly, who'd been making slow progress on the walk, three cows were following as if they wanted to annoy the little girl.

'Don't run,' shouted Dave, who began to move towards Sarah. 'They'll run after you if you do.' She controlled her pace and soon passed Dave to join Jim and Jo. Dave put his arms out and walked toward the cows, grunting as he did so. The cows came to a halt and, as Dave got near, one by one they turned and moved away. He glanced over his shoulder and waited until his friends had almost reached the gate at the edge of the field. Only then did he turn and walk slowly over to join them.

'They're harmless really,' he said. 'They're just incredibly curious, they'll follow anyone just to see what's going on.'

Once in the safety of the next field, Sarah left those at the back of the party and walked briskly—Molly running alongside her and clinging to her hand. She clearly wasn't pleased that her friends hadn't noticed her absence and were way ahead, deep in conversation.

'Jim, are you as uncertain about praying for the general needs of non-Christians, like their health, employment and general welfare, as you are about their salvation?' Dave asked.

'No, strange as it may seem, I don't find that a problem. There's plenty evidence of God's concern for people's welfare and our responsibility to pray and to do something for them.'[46]

'Any examples?' asked Dave.

'Well, just off the cuff, I can think of the command to leave the corners of the field after harvest for the widows and strangers;[47] God's concern for the Egyptians facing seven years of famine;[48] Amos's denunciation of the exploitation of the poor;[49] and, of course, Jesus's feeding of the multitude.[50] Some of these are specifically concerns for God's people, but others aren't. There are plenty other examples that make it clear God is concerned for humanity, so his welfare is surely a valid topic for prayer.'

'Mmm, there's a problem I have with your position, Jim. Can God be so concerned about man's daily needs that He invites us to pray about them, yet not so concerned about his eternal needs that He doesn't place this responsibility upon us, too?'

'I think you haven't quite understood me,' said Jim. 'There's no suggestion that there's no responsibility to pray for the unsaved; if there's no heartfelt prayer, there's something wrong with a Christian's spiritual life. What I'm trying to say is that the content of that prayer must be subject to biblical principles. My prayer at a personal level is that I'd live a life that not only commends the gospel but also takes the opportunities, even when that may be costly, to tell people about Christ. Such praying puts an even heavier responsibility for evangelism on me. I'm not allowed to ease my conscience with the thought that I haven't told people I know on the basis that I pray for them. But, when all that is done, and prayer has been made that the gospel might be made known clearly and convincingly, the final word in salvation is God's. My concern is that we pray more and in a way that acknowledges God to be sovereign—not one whose glory is dependent on the whims of man.'

Just then, Dave heard some excited talking ahead of him. He lifted his head from giving full concentration to Jim's reasoning. At the far side of the field the whole party had come to a halt, not knowing what their instructions were supposed to indicate. When Dave saw the dilemma, he immediately excused himself from Jim and Jo, and jogged off to sort out the confusion.

Questions to Ponder

1. What was affecting Becky's prayer life? What affects yours?
2. What biblical evidence show that God is concerned for the daily needs of life? How should this affect the Church's witness?
3. What should be the focus of praying for Christian friends and missionaries?
4. What did Jim say the solution is and is it appropriate for your own situation?

When the Going is Tough

Praying in the Barren Times

'I can see why Dave's such a proud father,' said Jim, as he bent over the crib to have a closer look at Josh.

'He's just like his Dad. You must be very proud of him, Becky.'

'He's a great joy,' she said rather flatly, looking down at Josh. 'It's hard to remember life without him.'

The sitting room door opened and a triumphant Dave put his head round, holding his hands at face height. They were covered with sludge.

'That drain stinks!' he said, laughing. 'But mission accomplished!'

Dave walked through to the kitchen, continuing to shout through to Jim and Becky as he scrubbed his hands. After a few minutes he reappeared, looking more serious.

'Thanks for coming round, Jim. We appreciate your time and wish we didn't have to bother you.'

'You're very welcome,' Jim said, as they all sat down. It was a beautiful summer's day and there was a welcome cooling breeze blowing through the open window; but Jim could sense that the new parents were struggling. Becky's mum and Dad had gone back home to Wales, and now she and Dave were coping with their first baby on their own.

'As I said to you on Sunday, it's not desperately urgent, but it's something we'd value your help on.

Nobody else seems to have our problem, so I'm loath to raise it in case they think we're going off the rails.'

'We're not doing that,' said Becky, 'but we are having great difficulty in adjusting.'

She glanced over to Josh, still sleeping peacefully.

'You've no idea,' she said, trying to smile. 'He seems to have turned our lives upside down, and there are times I wonder if I can cope with any extra demand beyond meeting his and Dave's needs.'

'Is he still waking up a lot at night?' asked Jim.

'That's the trouble,' said Dave. 'He sleeps well during the day, but he never seems to stop crying at night. Poor Becky is forever trying to satisfy him! The start of every day has become an effort of monumental proportions. We're both the sort that needs plenty of sleep; we just feel exhausted most of the time.'

Jim understood their problem more deeply than they realised. Not only did he know that other couples often faced it too, but he and Jo had done so themselves.

'Let me ask you,' he said, cutting to the chase, 'have you asked me round because it's playing on your spiritual lives?'

Becky suddenly burst into tears. It was totally unexpected. She'd appeared quite composed. Dave drew up along the settee beside her and put his arm around her to comfort her.

'I'm sorry, Jim,' she said. 'You must think I'm a poor specimen of victorious Christianity.'

'Do you think victorious living's all about fair-weather sailing?' he asked. 'It's in conditions like this that your commitment and faith are tried.'

'Yes, but I feel a total failure.'

'And so would all the other women I know if they had a baby who was demanding so much,' Jim replied reassuringly. 'Do you feel somehow responsible for Josh's temperament and unsettledness?' he asked.

Becky nodded.

'You know,' he went on, 'when Sophie was born, she was so good we thought we could write a book and tell the world how to make children happy and bring them up. People used to say such nice things to us like, 'It shows she knows she's loved', and so on. Then, when Emma arrived, we realised that Sophie's placid and friendly personality was no reflection on our abilities after all! She brought us down to earth with a real bump—and we needed it! Emma cried for England, and nothing we could do would settle her. At times, we were at our wit's end. There was nothing wrong with her, but it must have sounded to the neighbours that Jo and I were totally neglecting her! Emma made us realise our abilities at parenting were actually very shallow and how conceited we'd been with Sophie.'

'And here we thought there was a set of basic rules for bringing up children, and anyone with a difficult child was bearing the consequences of not sticking to them!' Becky laughed through her tears, in acknowledgement of their foolishness.

'Well,' said Jim, 'it's clear, you're making progress in the school of life! You're learning lessons that your degrees didn't teach you. Isn't that so?'

They both nodded.

'What other areas are you feeling the strain in?'

'Well, it seems to affect every part of our life,' said Dave 'For instance, we're very conscious of our tiredness when it comes to praying and reading our Bibles.'

'That's no surprise,' answered Jim; 'but I'm glad you're honest enough to say so. Do you know, to some degree, this is a problem that every Christian couple faces when they start a family. Being a parent is a tremendous responsibility and demands total attention at every hour of the day or night. If children have needs, you're the ones to see to them!'

'Don't I know it!' sighed Becky, looking over at the crib. 'I hadn't appreciated how Josh would be dependent on us for everything, absolutely everything.'

'And their needs change as they grow up,' said Jim. 'He'll no longer need you to wipe his nose, but he will need your love and understanding as he wrestles with his own problems. It's at this time, especially, that he's going to need your support and prayers.'

'That's where we're afraid,' Dave broke in. 'We both feel as though our prayer lives are slipping away. What sort of parents are we going to be when he gets to that age?'

'But, Dave,' said Jim, 'stop looking over your shoulder at what you were. You'll only cope with your new situation by accepting that God has new resources, new lessons and new purposes for you! What you need to do is adjust to it, without feeling guilty that you can't live as you did in the past.'

Suddenly, Josh became restless, his little arms trying to free him from the sheet that swaddled him. Becky went and stood over him, looking down helplessly and hoping he would settle.

'I think he had wind,' she whispered. 'Dave, could you carry him into the dining room so we don't wake him, and I'll make some tea.'

'That's a good idea,' he whispered, as he pulled himself up from the settee.

Soon the crib was carefully carried into the back room, and Dave, Becky and their pastor were relaxing over mugs of tea and chatting about different people they knew. A few names were mentioned of couples who no longer worshipped at Emmanuel.

'You know, I'm sure one of the main difficulties couples face, and one that causes some to stop following the Lord, is the stress of coping with family life, with all of its demands and conflict.'[51]

'Well that makes sense to me!' responded Becky dryly. 'I just didn't appreciate its pressures. Magazines and adverts give the impression it's all about fulfilment and happiness. They conveniently overlook the hard work and all the adjustments.'

'Let's get back to your spiritual upheaval in all this,' suggested Jim. 'I don't want you to think I've overlooked that.'

'Well ... is there anything we ought to be doing?' asked Dave.

'Before suggesting something you can do, it's a matter of coming to terms with your new situation. I've said already, I think a lot of couples go astray spiritually because they constantly look over their shoulder to how it was. They feel they've backslidden because they've not maintained what was an idealistic situation.'

Becky nodded. 'You're right, Jim. I often think about when we were students in Manchester. We were all just buzzing with serving the Lord—we lived for Him.'

'I know,' said Jim. 'I can remember my college days too. And do you realise what was special? Fellowship with God and His people was at the heart of everything, and that's where you must begin now.'

Becky bowed her head and Dave tensed, wondering what she was going to say. He recalled the number of times she'd screamed at him: 'I don't want to pray!' when he suggested that they should. It had gone on for such a long time and had seemed like a wedge that was being driven ever deeper into their marriage.

'Becky,' Jim said, watching her bite her lips, 'is there something on your mind? Has praying become a problem?'

She nodded her head slowly, putting her fingers over her mouth.

'It was building up before Josh was born; in fact, since we started going out together. My Christian life was so uncomplicated up to that point. There was nothing to distract me; it was just me and the Lord.'

'And you don't think you're really praying unless you can repeat those experiences?'

Again, she nodded her head.

'I want to pray like that again, but how can we?' she said, looking beseechingly at Dave, who knew exactly what she was referring to.

Jim felt he had to take the initiative. 'Becky, am I right in thinking there's something you feel really guilty about?' he asked, half looking at Dave to see his reaction too.

She swallowed hard.

'Yes, there is,' she said, averting his gaze. 'I feel crippled with guilt at times.'

'And that guilt makes you ashamed when you come to pray; you feel unclean and unworthy?'

Becky was fighting to keep her tears back and wiped the back of her hand across her eyes.

'Becky,' said Jim, 'I want you to know two things. Firstly, everyone has things of which they're deeply ashamed[52]; and, secondly, God knew what you would do before ever you failed Him, and loved you in spite of it. It made no difference to His love for you. If you insist on living in past guilt and shame, you're rejecting what He wants to give you.'[53]

'But it's no use,' she burst out. 'You don't understand!'

Dave's arm went around her and he pulled her close to his side, embarrassed that Jim was having an insight into a long-standing problem that they had, until that moment, succeeded in keeping private.

'Becky, I want you to listen to me carefully.'

She breathed deeply again.

'There's something you must understand. Not all guilt feelings are due to God accusing you. Satan also accuses Christians; that's why he's called the accuser of the brethren.'[54]

'But how do you know who's responsible?' Dave asked, anticipating Becky's question.

'Very simply,' Jim replied. 'The Holy Spirit never convicts us or makes us feel guilt for its own sake. He does it to bring us to experience God's remedy. His conviction leads us to know the joy of God's forgiveness and draws us near to Him.'[55]

Dave's eyes lit up.

'And Satan's accusations are made so that we feel so bad we're driven from God. So, our guilt shouldn't hold us back from praying!'

'Exactly,' replied Jim, clearly relieved that Dave had grasped the crux of the problem. 'Your remorse over your failure can't make you right with God. You must accept His love and forgiveness.'

'You mean,' responded Becky, 'Satan's been deceiving me all this time? God hasn't been rejecting me? He still really loves me?'

'He loves you no less than when He gave up His Son to die for you. Yes, He loves you, Becky, and wants you to love and trust Him.'

'Oh, do you know, hearing that makes me feel like I'm coming out of a long dark tunnel. At long last I feel clean; I don't need to pretend anymore!'

The strain had lifted and Becky lay back on the settee, looking up to the ceiling.

'I've lived in that darkness, Jim, for almost five years, and this is the first time I've really had peace in all that time.'

'Becky,' Jim said, 'I still think there are other issues to talk about as well. I don't want you to be overwhelmed by pressures that haven't been resolved.'

'Like what?' Dave chipped in.

'Well, you mentioned earlier how you've been totally exhausted since having Josh. I want to suggest something to you both.'

They listened attentively, holding each other's hands.

'You must support each other[56] and accept support from other people! Look, you need two things for balanced spiritual growth—and they might surprise you. You need to pray as a couple and you need to pray with God's people.'

'Trouble is, where do we get the time from?' Dave asked.

'You make yourselves time, with each other's help. Perhaps, once Josh is settled in an evening, you could spend time together reading the Bible and praying after your evening meal. And when you feel able to come out in an evening again you could take it in turns to come to the mid-week prayer meeting. It would be so good to have you and it's vital for you that you meet to pray with others from the church! Now, how about me setting you a challenge for your reading? How about you looking at the New Testament to see if you can find out how the apostles and early church prayed—it might help you to understand why I emphasised the importance of praying in the context of the church and not only praying on your own.'

The young parents looked at each other and couldn't contain their excitement. 'You're on, Jim; we'd like to do that!' It was clear they sensed this was a special opportunity to begin again.

Questions to Ponder

1. List the things that affect your prayer life.
2. Consider strategy's that could help you manage these factors.
3. What should our attitude be to changing circumstances in our lives that change our sense of wellbeing?

4. What are the strategies of Satan that you have experienced that have led you to think that God had withdrawn from you?
5. Why is praying with the church such an important principle?

DIY Prayer

Prayer and the Fellowship of Believers

The November day was bitingly cold and Jim fell to the ground panting—his whole body aching from the stress he'd put it through for the last hour. Drenched with sweat, he lay flat on his back, wondering what mad impulse had persuaded him to be involved in such a ridiculous attempt at glory. After a few minutes, he rolled over to see where the laughter was coming from.

'I'll never agree to play against the young people ever again!' he groaned.

'What's wrong?' Dave teased. 'Feeling your age?'

Dave had also been in the game, but knew his limitations and only played in the second half. His asthma made him pace himself carefully. Jim, on the other hand, had no concept of pacing himself and looked as though he would need oxygen to get through the next ten minutes.

'Feeling my age?' he replied, 'I feel it ten times over!'

Dave sat down beside him, and soon the tactics of the game were being analysed and evaluated.

'We started too quickly,' Jim admitted. 'Within five minutes we were in a fool's paradise with those two early goals.'

Dave laughed. From his position as a full back he'd seen the whole team run itself into the ground in the second half and had been helpless to stop the young people coming back with vengeance to win 9–2.

'It was a massacre. I don't think I dare face them from the pulpit tomorrow,' Jim joked. 'I'll have to use it as an illustration of perseverance … Talking of perseverance, how've things been since I came to see you? Have things got easier for Becky?'

'Yes, thanks Jim. She's so much more positive about things. We're not free of problems, but we're definitely moving forward. And we're seeing that our lives are not complete unless we're consciously caring and loving each other.'

'And you're finding that this is changing your attitude to other matters?'

'Yes, I think it is,' replied Dave. 'I just hope it's not a bubble that's going to burst! Since talking to you, we've begun to see our mutual dependence. We're trying to think of ourselves as two people sharing one life, caring for Josh and each other. And we're praying together each evening and reading the Bible as you suggested. We're learning!'

'That's great,' responded Jim. 'Mutual care is essential for any marriage to work. The trouble is most of us take a long time to discover that marriage isn't just a legal contract or a respectable way of cohabiting. It really is about two people becoming one … How else are you seeing things differently?'

'Well, I think we're learning how to cope with our weaknesses and failings. We'd been living a sort of artificial existence. We knew about the principles of marriage but didn't know how to live them out. We felt we knew what we should be and couldn't cope with what we really were. It made for a relationship that was very strained at times. Now we feel much more comfortable together, and we're beginning to see how we help or hinder each other … One thing that has cropped up is the whole matter of "quiet times" and private prayer. We're thinking we need to go back to square one on that one and would welcome your thoughts.'

'That's interesting,' smiled Jim. 'Is this a result of your studies? Go on then, what sort of ideas have you had?'

'Well,' began Dave tentatively, afraid he'd offend his pastor with the conclusions they'd come to from their reading, 'we've been asking ourselves if our "quiet times" have often just been rituals, and even whether they're what Scripture actually says we should be concerned about.'[57]

'Interesting! Are you questioning the value of prayer and Bible reading?' Jim probed, delighted that his young friends were trying so hard to understand what the Scriptures were saying.

'No, not at all!' Dave assured him. 'They're vital. What we're questioning is how we hear God's Word and how we pray. Do you know, Jim, I don't think the intensely personal emphasis we had was right after all, even though it seemed so wonderful when we were students. We've tried to do what you told us to do—to check everything by the Scriptures, and, in spite of looking, we just don't get the impression there was a "quiet time" structure in the early church.'

'Let me ask you, Dave: are you beginning to think that your spiritual difficulties are partly due to conforming to a particular pattern or practice—somehow you've had the wrong sort of spiritual diet?'

'Yes, I think that's probably what I am thinking.'

'But you're not questioning the importance of prayer and Bible reading?'

'Absolutely not,' said Dave, emphatically shaking his head. 'That's not crossed our minds. Becky and I want to read our Bibles more and pray more, but we're just not sure how this should develop to keep it in line with the New Testament.'

'In what way do you think it could develop?'

'Well, we were wondering if our Bible reading and prayer could be more of a corporate experience—something that involved all of us at Emmanuel.'

'Sorry to disturb you sportsmen, I thought you'd like some coffee and sandwiches.'

It was Becky, who'd pushed Josh in his buggy round to the common and across to where Jim and Dave were sitting.

'Hello,' beamed Dave. 'I didn't hear you coming up behind us. I thought you were staying at home!'

'I was', said Becky, 'but Josh has done nothing but cry. I thought it might help to get him out the house.'

She sat down beside the men and began to unpack the picnic she'd prepared. They pounced on it like hungry hounds.

'What were you talking about?'

'I was just sharing with Jim our thoughts about quiet times.'

Becky smiled. 'Do you think we're going off the rails?'

'Not at all! I think you've touched a raw nerve that needs to be exposed. In the West, we prize our individualism that the Enlightenment brought; but one of the prices we paid was a loss of the corporate dimension of Christian truth. We often forget that the West is out of step with the rest of the world—some people groups emphasise the community before the individual, whilst we emphasise the individual before the community. And … I'm freezing! Tell you what, shall we walk round to the church and finish off in the lounge?'

The young couple and Jim gathered their things together and began to wander off the common and round to the church, Josh still sleeping soundly in his buggy.

'Jim, what was the Enlightenment?' asked Becky. 'I've heard it mentioned on TV, but no one's said what it was.'

'Well, it was a period in Western history in the eighteenth century, when all the values and ideas that'd been accepted as true were thrown into the melting pot by the philosophers. It changed the way Europeans thought. Its effect was to put reason above all other forms of authority. It soon meant that the authority of the church, and of God himself, was being challenged. Because it emphasised human reason as the final court of appeal, it had a knock-on effect of emphasising and exalting the individual. It was good that people were free to think for themselves; but it resulted in fragmented societies, where individuals were more important than the societies they belonged to.'

'Don't Jews emphasise the family and community before the individual?'

'They do, Becky, and this reflects the influence of the Old Testament Scriptures on their value system,' responded Jim.

Dave was quick to make the connections: 'Are you saying that the Enlightenment could have robbed us of the Biblical view of humanity? It would make sense, because we looked up "man" in a theological dictionary and found that the concept was far more corporate than we realised. It said it was important to rediscover the Biblical perspective for all sorts of reasons.'

'And I think that's absolutely right! Getting back to your concern about individual quiet times, what did you find out about the way the apostles and the early church prayed and read the Scriptures?'

'Well, it just seemed so different from what we've been used to. I wonder if our structure's artificial, limiting what the Holy Spirit wants to do,' said Dave, tentatively.

'How do you mean?'

'Well, I didn't find anywhere that they had daily "quiet times"! It's clear they prayed—their lives were lived in an atmosphere of prayer—but the emphasis seemed to be far more on corporate prayer than private. I guess both were there, but the dominant pattern was definitely the corporate one.'[58]

'Which fits in with what you've said about the corporate nature of man!' responded Jim. 'You know, there are still many countries where the church puts a great deal of emphasis on believers meeting together to pray, and the spiritual quality of their lives is high. Interestingly, all these countries emphasise man's corporate nature. But how about Bible reading? What did you find out about that?'

'Well, the same really—we just didn't find an emphasis on personal Bible reading.'

'I suppose that's not surprising,' responded Jim. 'The early believers didn't possess Bibles. In fact, it's only been in the past few hundred years that Bibles could be printed, and it's only been in the past 150 years that most people in the West could afford them. So, the early Christians couldn't possibly have had the type of private daily Bible reading we have today.'

'Of course, I never thought of that! I suppose it would mean the only way they could know more about the Scriptures was to gather together and have them read to them—it was impossible for the early church to have been individualistic in its study of the Scriptures.'

'Absolutely, and gathering together to have the Scriptures read to them and explained by the apostles would have ensured the integrity of their understanding. This would have been why Calvin held daily meetings—the people came every day to the church in Geneva for instruction. Can you imagine having daily worship and being taught by a giant like Calvin?'

At last, they reached the church, and were soon continuing in the welcome warmth of the lounge.

Becky picked up the conversation: 'Then, what was happening under Calvin's leadership at Geneva was just like what would have been happening in Jerusalem, when the disciples met each day for instruction. Did the advent of personal Bible reading replace corporate worship and learning, to the detriment of the church? Funnily enough, I find it's much easier to pray with others than when I'm alone. Perhaps that's because God made me to be part of a community, especially the community of the church?'

'So, are we wrong in reading the Bible privately at all?' Dave asked.

'No, of course not!' said Jim. 'But I think we can learn something really important, and useful, from the early church. The Christians were obviously dependent on hearing the Scriptures read to them. They were also told to let the Word of God dwell in them richly. That must have entailed memorising it—they were memorising key Scriptures in the context of the gathered church! So, they were being taught their significance by the apostles—whom Jesus had given authority to teach—and committing them to memory.'

Jim suddenly reflected on what he'd just said and how it didn't match up to what was happening in Emmanuel at that time.

'Really,' he said, 'we ought to try to get back to the apostolic and reformation pattern here as much as possible. That doesn't mean we shouldn't have Bible study and prayer at home, but we should probably have it in order to reinforce what's being taught in the church at the time. That places a big responsibility on any pastor, but I think I could go along with it—I can certainly see lots of biblical and historical grounds for doing so.'

'And I think it'd resolve the feelings of frustration and failure we struggle with when we try to go it alone,' said Dave. 'Our praying and Bible reading need relocating into, as you say, the context of the gathered church. I wonder if our problem's been that we've been trying to fit a square peg into a round hole—trying to make isolated Christians fit into the corporate mould of the New Testament. It doesn't work for the simple reason the New Testament knows nothing of solitary Christianity!'

'So, Jim, remind us again what the early church did that we, possibly, don't do.'

'Well, Becky, they memorised God's Word—they had to because they didn't have their own copies to read. They were saturated with Scripture! Secondly, they had a greater sense of its authority because it wasn't a private matter of interpretation—they appreciated that God had given teachers to His people and they accepted their instruction. This minimised the sort of fragmentation we have today, where people insist that God has spoken to them through passages that are quoted out of context. And thirdly, they had a tremendously positive attitude toward the Christian community. They understood its importance for their lives and knew it was where God intended them to be taught and supported. We miss so much of this when we emphasise a private spirituality. Do you know, our method would fit comfortably into privatisation and the dismantling of community structures.'

'This sounds like an expanded version of our earlier conversation when I said Becky and I were learning that we're not two independent people, struggling to exist in a marriage relationship; we're two people, sharing one life and giving each other mutual support. I wonder if the problem with a church like Emmanuel is that we're a group of largely stand-alone Christians with private experiences rather than members of the same body sharing the same life?'

'Do you know, when I think of it,' said Jim, 'the most thrilling time of my Christian life was when I went to the prayer meetings and Bible studies back in Liverpool. I was only a young believer, but I'd go home from those meetings and study for hours what I'd been introduced to by the pastor. The impact on my praying was profound too; and I think I could see more clearly what God's purposes were. Sadly, with our DIY spirituality, we've become isolated from this. To my shame, I've got to say that Emmanuel has! Everyone's reading whatever they want from the Bible at home, interpreting it as they see fit; and praying on their own, too. Our corporate experience is so paltry! Oh, we come together on Sunday mornings for teaching, but we mostly sing individualistic worship songs. Some, like yourselves, come to the mid-week meeting for prayer and Bible study, but most clearly don't think they need it! Mmm ... I need to do some serious thinking.'

'But we're not the early church,' responded Becky, concerned that her pastor was being discouraged. 'They lived in a different society and culture. They weren't slogging it out in a modern economy, where men go out to work just after seven in the morning and are doing a short day if they get back to eat with their families in the evening. Isn't the problem that we're forced to live these individualistic lifestyles? Can the sort of corporate life enjoyed by the early church really be achieved today in Emmanuel?'

'I'm painfully aware of how right you are,' responded Jim. 'The pace of life and the demands of our lifestyles do seem, at times, to pull us apart. But there's no getting away from it, we do need to ask some fundamental questions about what God's will is for us. You know, if we're willing to evaluate what we do in the light of its eternal worth and make appropriate changes, we could, as a fellowship, begin to move in the right direction—it could be very, very exciting!'

Questions to Ponder

1. What is the Enlightenment and how has it changed the west?
2. What was the context of the early church's teaching what value did it have?
3. What is the danger of a private spirituality? Can it ever be justified?
4. What makes corporate worship and prayer difficult for many in the twenty first century?
5. Suggest ways the corporate precedence could be fostered.

Burnt Custard and a Crying Baby

Praying in the Spirit

Jim and Jo stood on the step, waiting for someone to answer the bell. It was a bitter winter's night, but it felt good to be away from the house for a few hours together. Dave and Becky had decided to thank Jim for his help over the past year by inviting them round for a meal before Christmas.

'Isn't it lovely, Jim, just to be away from the phone for a few hours. Do you know,' she said, 'I feel quite excited.'

Jim smiled. He could see, without her saying it, that she was beginning to relax.

'Mind you, it's not going to be all pleasure.'

'It will for me,' whispered Jo, as she heard someone coming to the door.

She knew what he meant. Dave had invited several others as well and had asked Jim to lead a discussion on prayer after the meal.

The door opened and, to Jim's surprise, it was Tom.

'Hello,' he said with a warm smile. 'Lovely to see you again! Dave is just settling Josh and Becky's trying to rescue some burnt custard, so I've taken over as the official welcomer!'

Smiling, Jim and Jo stepped into the hall and heard chattering and laughter coming from the lounge. Jo opened the door and immediately two of Dave's guests, Rob and Doug, stood up to welcome her.

'Hi!' she smiled, 'and hello girls,' she said warmly to their wives, Rachel and Sarah. They were two lovely young couples—Rob and Rachel were a great help to Jim in promoting what the church was doing in the community, and Doug and Sarah were great personal workers and encouragers among the young people.

'As you can see,' said Tom, following Jim into the room, 'I'm the sensible one.'

'In what way could you possibly be that, Tom?' laughed Jim.

'Well, I'm the only one who's maintained his freedom!'

Soon the Thompsons were part of the conversation and very relaxed with the younger members of their congregation.

'Who's looking after the children?' Jo asked Sarah and Rachel.

'Oh! Bethan and Natalie,' answered Rachel. 'Becky didn't just invite us to a meal but she also arranged babysitters!'

'Actually, it's made the evening extra special,' said Sarah, 'because I really hate asking people to babysit in case it's putting them out. Are Sophie and Emma OK?'

'Yes, you know what it's like: Sophie's cramming hard for her mocks next month and Emma's trying hard not to do her homework! We've left Gran in charge—she'll sort them out!'

Just then, Dave appeared.

'Great to see you all,' he said, 'and I'm sorry we've been such lousy hosts, but Josh didn't settle as quickly as I'd hoped. Anyway, Becky's standing at the ready with her burnt custard, so perhaps you'd come through for the grub!'

Soon, everyone—especially Tom—was piling food onto their plates and tucking into Becky's lasagne; even the burnt custard didn't spoil her apple pie too much!

'Becky, that was a wonderful meal,' said Jim.

Other comments of approval and praise poured from the guests, leaving Becky quietly relieved and surprised that everything had gone so well.

'Let's go next door and grab some comfier seats. Leave the dishes on the table,' said Dave, 'and I'll do them later.'

After lots of protests, the friends finally submitted to his insistence that the evening should be used for other purposes. Soon they were all settled in the living room. It was lit by the Christmas tree in the corner and festooned with decorations in anticipation of Josh's first Christmas. Into this happy atmosphere, Becky carried a tray of coffee to finish off their meal.

'I'm looking forward to this discussion,' she said, as she handed Jim a coffee.

'Yes,' said Tom. 'When Dave told me you'd talk to us about praying in the Spirit, it sounded intriguing!'

'Well,' laughed Jim, as he stirred his coffee, 'it's a very big subject. Perhaps to start things off I could ask you all what you think praying in the Spirit is.'

Rob was the first to respond. 'I think it's prayer that is somehow so intense you know you're in a spiritual battle.'

'Could it be praying when you're constrained to pray—you know, when you can't help but pray for someone or something,' said Rachel.

Jim waited a moment, nodding in assent to what Rob and Rachel had said.

'I think ...' said Tom cautiously, 'I think there's an element in which we sense the mind of God and are helped, by the Spirit, to pray with a supernatural confidence.'

'Good,' said Jim. 'Do you see how there are different ways we can pray in the Spirit? I'd like to suggest it's even more than these.'

Jim stretched forward, put his mug on the glass coffee table in front of him and took hold of his Bible.

'One of the first things we need to do is distinguish between praying in the Holy Spirit and praying in the spirit.'

He smiled. 'Oh, dear! I can see I've puzzled you already! I don't want to give you verbal indigestion after that lovely meal, but it's important you understand the difference.'

'I just thought they were different ways of saying the same thing,' admitted Doug, shrugging his shoulders.

'Most people do, Doug; but there does seem to be a distinction in the New Testament. I think we'd better start if that's OK with you?'

Everyone agreed, so Jim continued. 'First we need to understand that there is more than one spirit in the New Testament. There are evil spirits, of course, but there's also the human spirit. It's the references to the human spirit that are difficult to identify, because sometimes a passage can refer to the Holy Spirit and sometimes to the spirit of man.'

'Isn't that what you said months ago, when you were preaching in Romans 8?' asked Becky. 'Didn't you say then that, because Greek writing didn't have capitals in Paul's day, you could only judge what spirit was being referred to by carefully examining the passage?'

'That's right!' beamed Jim, 'and full marks for remembering that! We get this confusion in Acts—Apollos is described as being fervent in the spirit, yet he's clearly not a believer.'[59]

'I can't understand that,' said Sarah. 'How could he be fervent in the spirit—or even just have the spirit—and not be a Christian?'

Jim didn't want to give an immediate answer. He waited to see if any of the others would make a suggestion.

'Could it be ...' Becky said hesitantly, 'could it be a reference to his enthusiasm for the message he preached, however incomplete his understanding was?'

'That would make sense,' Dave added, proudly.

'It would,' agreed Jim, 'because the spirit can't refer to the Holy Spirit in Apollos's case as He only indwells believers.'

Jim eased back into his armchair, worried that he was losing the concentration of his young friends. 'You see, it's possible to pray in the Spirit, capital "S", and in the spirit, small "s"? Let me ask you two questions. First, what do you think is the difference between these two types of praying?'

'One is God-inspired and the other is man-inspired,' suggested Tom.

'Absolutely!' said Jim. 'Now, the next question: when somebody's praying, how can we distinguish between the two?'

There was an uneasy silence for a few moments and Jo wished she could come to her husband's aid by saying something helpful. It was clear that this was not so simple a question.

'Well, let me ask you: if we were to have a time of prayer now and I prayed something like: "Please, Lord, send Your Son back to this earth at nine o'clock tomorrow", how would you react?'

'I'd feel very uncomfortable because I'd know you weren't praying in God's will,' said Rob. 'Jesus said no one knows the hour He's going to return.'[60]

'So, how can you judge if a prayer is prayed in the Spirit?'

'Got it!' responded Rob, with excitement. 'You know it is if it's in harmony with God's Word. The Holy Spirit won't inspire a prayer that conflicts with the truth He caused to be written!'

Much to Jo's relief, there was consent to this from the rest of the group. They relaxed, and some offered examples of times when they'd heard people pray and it was clear their prayers were unanswerable because they'd have caused God to break His own word.

'Do you see,' asked Jim, 'if we become divorced from Scripture, we could allow all manner of romantic spiritual sentiments develop in our understanding? These would eventually have the disastrous effect of supplanting Scripture in our thinking. We must always be on our guard against this.'

Just then, Jim noticed a look on Becky's face he knew only too well. She glanced over to Dave, who immediately got up and quickly moved towards the door. Everyone stopped talking as though some momentous event was about to happen! He stepped into the hall and looked up to the top of the stairs. As Josh cried it seemed Dave was holding his breath in case it made too much noise. After a minute or so he turned back to his guests and smiled, saying, 'Phew! He's settled down again. Sorry about that.'

'Good old Josh!' said Tom, generously. 'Getting back to praying in the Spirit and what you said about man-inspired prayer, isn't it possible to pray about things that are in harmony with Scripture and yet not in harmony with what God wants?'

'How do you mean?'

'Well, I was thinking of that passage where the writer says there's a sin that's "unto death", and he goes on to say that his readers are not to pray for a person who has committed this sin.'[61]

'That's right,' replied Jim. 'So it's obvious that praying in the Spirit is more than just being theologically correct.'

Sarah had listened intently to what had been a mostly male-dominated discussion, trying to stay in touch with what had been said. She sat leaning forward, with her elbows on her knees and her chin in her hands.

'So, Jim,' she said, 'what is praying in the Spirit?'

He laughed. 'Sarah, you haven't been satisfied with discovering what it's not, have you? And I must confess it is easier to say what it's not rather to say what it is! I'll try to explain what I think it is, and I'll do it under three headings.'

'Sounds like a good sermon!' teased Dave, and everyone laughed when Jim apologised for being so predictable.

'Well, here's my first point. Praying in the Spirit must involve praying for things we're told to pray about.'

'Such as?' asked Rachel.

'Well, Paul tells Timothy to pray for those who rule over us.[62] Can anyone think of anything else?'

'How about evangelism,' suggested Rob. 'Jesus did say to pray for the Lord of the harvest to send labourers into His harvest.'[63]

'Exactly right, Rob, and if you look at 1 Timothy 2 you'll see that one reason we're to pray for peace and stability is so that the gospel will not be obstructed. Can you think of any other examples of "responsible" praying?'

'How about praying for our families—their safety and conversion if they're not Christians?' asked Rachel.

'Yes, I'd have thought so, although it's inferred rather than actually commanded in Scripture. After all, if a man is worse than an infidel when he doesn't provide for his family,[64] he'd be worse still if he didn't pray for them!'

'Didn't Job pray for his children?'[65] chipped in Sarah. 'And Jesus said to bring the children to Him because the kingdom of God belonged to such as them.'[66]

'You're right, Sarah,' encouraged Jo. 'And there were all those times when people in need were brought to Jesus,[67] as well as those who appealed to Him themselves.'[68]

'Surely the Lord's prayer will show us what we should be praying for,' said Tom. 'After all, it was given as a model for the disciples to follow.'[69]

'Excellent idea,' said Jim. 'And what do you think those things are, Tom?'

He was ready with his answer, his mind having already scanned the prayer. 'Well, the expansion of

God's kingdom; the glorifying of His name; our daily needs; our forgiveness; and our protection from Satan's attacks.'

'That's pretty comprehensive, Tom! Do you know, if we began to pray about those things, many aspects of our lives, and the lives of other people, would be touched.'

Jim then turned to Doug and said, 'Can you pinpoint one last example for us, Doug?'

'Well, how about praying for people who're going through testing times that their faith won't fail—like the Christians in North Korea?'

Everybody agreed that praying for persecuted Christians around the world should come close to the top of their prayer requests and were ashamed how late in the discussion they remembered them.

'Well, now let's look at a second aspect of praying in the Spirit. It's the only reference to the Spirit actually helping us in prayer. It's in Romans 8.'

Lifting his Bible from the coffee table, Jim soon found the chapter. 'Listen to what Paul says: "The Spirit helps us in our weakness. We do not know what we ought to pray for, but the Spirit himself intercedes for us with groans that words cannot express. And he who searches our hearts knows the mind of the Spirit, because the Spirit intercedes for the saints in accordance with God's will."[70] Can I ask how many of you would think that praying in the Spirit would be some sort of incredibly exhilarating experience?'

Several nodded.

'Well, I've got news for you. If you look at what comes before this statement, you'll see Paul is writing about the certainty of weakness, corruption and death.[71] He says that the whole of creation is longing for a deliverance from its bondage and agony. Hardly an exhilarating experience! Then we come to this statement, where he says we don't even know what to pray for but the Spirit helps us with inexpressible groanings.'

Becky sat pondering the implications of this for a few moments, then said: 'Jim, do you think it could refer to those times we feel we're being dragged along backwards by the world and our circumstances, and become desperately alarmed by our lack of spirituality? When I wake up to that sort of situation, I feel so weak and tell God that He must do something for me. Sometimes I'm ashamed at speaking to God in this way because I feel such a hypocrite; but I just feel distressed with an inner longing.'

'That's right, Becky. I'm sure we lose sight of important biblical teaching when we think praying in the Spirit is some sort of spiritual Cruise missile! Its effects are more powerful than anything we imagine; but it's nothing to do with the power of our praying, it's to do with the power of God. And what moves Him like nothing else is the frailty and need of His people who turn to Him, broken and conscious of their weakness.'

'Do you know,' said Tom, 'seeing it that way is quite different from the way I've seen it before. If I understand you and the Scriptures right, we're praying in the Spirit when we're on the edge of despair over what we are or what we can do; and we put it before God, as He alone can meet our need.'

Sarah admitted: 'I think I've done more praying in the Spirit than I've realised! I always felt bad about times of prayer like that, thinking that, if I really was close to God, I'd be a very different Christian—always happy and victorious!'

'Not necessarily happy,' said Jim, 'but certainly dependent … totally dependent.'

'What was the third area of praying in the Spirit, Jim?' asked Dave.

'Strangely, it's the one where joy is present. It's to do with praying through persecution and praying others through to spiritual maturity.'

'Before you come on to that,' Becky chipped in, 'I'll put the kettle on for another drink.'

'I'll give you a hand, Becky,' offered Sarah, as she pulled herself out of her chair.

Within five minutes they'd reappeared with a couple of trays filled with the orders they'd taken.

The mugs were soon passed around and Jim, aware of how time was passing and the need for babysitters to be relieved, soon got the topic back on track.

'Now then,' he continued, 'praying for Christians facing persecution. Do you know, there's more about this type of praying than any other in the entire New Testament!'

'Really? I thought most praying was about healing.'

'That's understandable, Tom. The amount of interest in healing might suggest that it is the New Testament's priority, but that doesn't square up with the biblical facts.'

'What passage are you thinking of?' asked Rob.

'There're really so many that it's difficult to isolate a particular one, but I think Paul's request for prayer in Ephesians 6 is a good one to start with. Listen to this: "And pray in the Spirit on all occasions with all kinds of prayers and requests. With this in mind, be alert and always keep on praying for all the saints. Pray also for me, that whenever I open my mouth, words may be given me so that I will fearlessly make known the mystery of the gospel, for which I am an ambassador in chains. Pray that I may declare it fearlessly, as I should."[72] Do you see,' asked Jim, 'how Paul can't separate praying in the Spirit from praying for believers to be helped in their persecution?'

'That's something I'd never noticed before,' commented Dave. 'It's interesting that Paul's not asking for them to pray for his deliverance but that he'll be kept faithful.'

'That's right,' agreed Doug, flicking through Paul's other letters in his Bible. 'His own safety doesn't seem to concern him at all, does it? His plea is always to be made fearless to preach the gospel.'

'He seems to link praying in the Spirit with being strengthened by the Spirit … I suppose in this way he can overcome the forces of evil that want to stop the spread of the gospel,' suggested Rachel.

'Rachel,' beamed Jim, punching the arm of his chair, 'You've got it exactly! Paul exhorts believers regularly to pray over all kinds of matters; but almost every letter he writes refers to the vital need for believers to pray that others, as well as themselves, will resist the pressure to be silent. This is the most vital type of praying.'[73]

'You said this type of praying is linked with joy. How can that be?' asked Sarah.

'Well, if you examine Paul's prayers, you'll see over and over again the joy he has in seeing his friends stand, despite terrible opposition.[74] But there's also Jesus's own promise to those who're suffering that they'll know inexpressible joy in bearing witness to Him, regardless of what it costs them.'[75]

'It seems you feel deeply concerned about this type of praying, Jim,' commented Dave.

He nodded. 'I have to confess that I think the devil sometimes laughs at some of our prayer meetings. This is where spiritual battles are lost or won![76] When we concentrate on praying about our own whims and wishes rather than coming to grips with this realm of spiritual conflict, we're like soldiers being concerned about the colour of blankets they've been issued rather than the enemy who's about to blow them up.'

'But don't you think we should pray about the everyday detail of our lives?' Doug asked.

'Yes, as long as it's in the context of an everyday concern to see Satan's power in people's lives brought to an end. If our praying is about guidance for colour schemes in the bathroom—and I've known some to see involving God in this way to be a mark of spirituality—then, as I said, I can't but believe that the devil laughs at us.'

Time had passed, and the evening was brought to an end. Jim prayed for them all and their families as they parted; and soon Dave and Becky stood at their front door, waving as the last of the cars pulled away from the pavement.

Becky shivered. 'Let me see,' said Dave, as he put his arm around her. 'Praying in the Spirit is prayer that is governed by scriptural guidelines ... that senses its weakness ... and is concerned about the witness of the church. I think we're going to have to work at this.'

Questions to Ponder

1. What does praying in the Spirit mean to you?
2. Why do we have to be careful about interpreting the meaning of the use of the term Spirit (or spirit) in the New Testament?
3. What are we commanded to pray about?
4. What principles should guide us about praying for healing?

5. What are the things that we should pray about?

Prayer in a Senseless World

Prayer When the Darkness is Tangible

Jim swung quickly into the car park. It'd been a terrible journey. He still couldn't take it in. He'd heard from Jo just as he was leaving the committee meeting in London. The news had made him shake physically.

He'd abandoned his plans to stay for refreshments and had driven for the last two hours, feeling helpless and fearful of what he was going to find when he arrived at the hospital.

Within minutes he was parked, locked up and was walking through the hospital's main entrance. He made his way over to the reception.

'I understand a family was brought in this afternoon. They've been involved in a road accident,' he said, shakily.

'What's the name?'

'Knight, David and Rebecca Knight. They have a son, Joshua.'

'There's no record of a David and Rebecca Knight being admitted,' the receptionist said, 'but a Joshua Knight was admitted earlier today. Could that be him? He's on the Children's Ward. That's on Level One.'

Jim thanked her and hurried to the ward. Level One was on the lower ground floor, so there was little point in waiting for the lift. He paced down the stairs, along a maze of drab corridors, until he came to the double door that led to the Children's Ward. It was locked. It seemed an age before anyone came to open it. He hurried down the corridor, still festooned with Christmas decorations yet to be taken down, and came to the desk—his heart beating quickly as he wondered what he was going to find. He hadn't been able to understand why Josh was a patient when his parents were not. The awful thought had crossed his mind that it might be because they were dead.

A young nurse sat studying her computer screen. She looked up at Jim as she heard him approaching and, smiling, she asked, 'Can I help you?'

'Yes, I'm the minister of Joshua Knight who I believe was admitted this afternoon. Can you give me any news? Do you know anything of the parents?'

The nurse's expression changed. 'Oh,' she said, 'Joshua's in theatre. His parents will be so glad to see you. They're in the visitors' room, just over there.'

Jim thanked her and, flooded with relief that they'd survived, he walked towards the door.

It was one of those pastors' nightmares. Images of a mutilated child went through his mind, and he felt sick at the thought of what Dave and Becky must be trying to cope with. His mind was in turmoil with the thought of the questions he'd have to try to answer.

When he got to the door, he could see Dave and Becky through its small glass window. They were sitting on a settee, holding hands. They looked utterly exhausted and shocked, and had obviously been through an awful ordeal. He pushed the door slowly, and they both looked up.

'Jim!' they said spontaneously. In seconds, they were huddled together in the centre of the room. Tears began to flow, first from Becky and then from Dave.

'Oh, Jim!' Becky cried. 'These have been the worst hours of our lives. We can't take it in.' She sobbed and sobbed.

Jim made no response. He couldn't. It would have been an intrusion into their grief. They stood huddled together for what seemed like several minutes.

'Come and sit down,' he eventually said, taking his arms away from them. Dave and Becky sat down again, and Jim pulled a chair up to face them.

'What happened? I was in London when Jo phoned to say you'd been involved in an accident. I came as soon as I could.'

'She's been marvellous,' responded Becky. 'We don't know what we'd have done without her.'

'Jo's been phoning every hour to see how we are, and she's phoned Becky's parents to break the news to them. They're driving up from South Wales now,' added Dave.

'But what happened? Jo wasn't sure about much when we spoke. Is there any news of Josh?'

'He's in theatre,' responded Becky. 'We're so worried; they're doing tests. They're not sure about the extent of his injuries.' Becky started sobbing again, and Dave put his arm around her.

'Jim,' he sighed, 'we really can't take it in. I had the day off work and we went shopping. We were crossing the junction when an oil tanker came through the lights on red. We didn't stand a chance. He hit the back of us, and we spun round into the path of another car that hit us. We couldn't believe we were still alive. Then we realised that Josh wasn't crying—he was slumped over in his car seat. He was still breathing, but was absolutely motionless. It seemed hours before the ambulance came.'

'What time was the accident?'

'Just after lunch, about 1.30,' responded Dave.

'How long has Josh been in theatre?'

'It must be about three hours. They had to do scans and tests before they took him down and that took time.'

The conversation faded. It's not easy to talk over trivialities in circumstances like these. Jim broke the silence by asking if they minded him phoning Jo to let her know he'd arrived. They both assured him they were alright, so he walked out of the ward into the bleak corridor.

'It's Jim. I got here about half an hour ago. Josh is very ill and He's still in theatre; Becky's parents are on their way up from Cardiff.'

'Everyone's so upset,' Jo responded. 'We're all so stunned. I keep bursting into tears.'

He assured her that Becky and Dave seemed alright and told her he intended to stay some time. 'Don't wait up for me,' he said, 'I think I'll be out pretty late.'

Jim walked slowly back to the ward. He could only guess what Dave and Becky were going through. He thought of the road ahead for them. He knew that if Josh didn't survive, there would be indescribable pain and a long dark road through depression. He'd never known a parent who'd lost a child not to go along that road. 'It's the most painful loss possible,' he thought to himself. But if Josh survives, what condition will he be in? How are Dave and Becky going to cope?

'Jo sends her love,' he said, as he walked into the room. 'She's getting dozens of calls. The folk at church are very concerned for you all. They're getting together tonight at the manse to pray for Josh.'

Dave and Becky smiled in acknowledgement.

Jim sat down in the chair. He was about to say something to make conversation in an attempt to occupy their minds, when Dave said, 'Jim, I don't think I know how to pray. It feels so dark—there's no light.'

'The Spirit prays with groanings that can't be uttered,' Becky reminded him as she put her head on his shoulder. 'It's not the words that we say that matter,' she whispered, 'it's the cry of our hearts that matters.'

Jim was surprised at this response. It seemed so often that Becky relied on Dave; and, yet, here she was, rising above what Jim had seen crush other mothers.

She turned to him: 'I don't think I've ever felt like this before. It may just be shock, showing itself in some bizarre way. But now I have an incredible sense of peace.'

The two men glanced at each other. Probably, they were thinking the same thought: 'How would she cope if the doctor walked through the door and started his sentence with: "I'm very sorry ..."? '

The silence in the room returned. It was tangible. They seemed to be wrapped up in their own thoughts. Jim was struggling within himself, not knowing how best to help them.

'Would you like me to pray with you for Josh?' Jim asked. He feared his sense of unease was obvious. Dave's comment on not knowing how to pray seemed to have influenced him.

They bowed their heads, and the pastor started to search for words that would be helpful, as well as real, before God.

'Father, You know that we're in such pain, fear and darkness. We don't know how to begin to ask You for Josh. You know what's best for him, and You know what we want; but we can't turn the clock back. Oh, that we could! Please, in Your infinite mercy, give the surgeons wisdom, and help them do what's right for him. Please Father, make Yourself known to Dave and Becky, and help them be strong. Help them find the power of Your love in this darkness. Amen.'

Jim heard faint whispers of 'Amen'.

Dave raised his head and looked over to him. 'I think all those talks on prayer are being put into practice,' he said. 'I feel so incredibly weak. I don't know how I'll cope if Josh doesn't come through.'

Jim looked at them. 'If it helps, I've some idea what you're going through.'

The response was virtually non-existent.

'I do have some idea,' Jim repeated, gently. 'Did you know that Jo isn't my first wife?'

They couldn't take it in. They'd always thought that he and Jo were so happy, and that Jim, somehow, had a privileged insurance policy, specially drawn up in heaven—one that protected him from sorrow. It had never occurred to them that he'd known any real pain.

'Helen and I married just after I graduated from theological college,' Jim continued. 'She was wonderful. We were so very happy. It was on the eve of our first wedding anniversary that Helen began to feel unwell. She went to the doctor's, and phoned me from the surgery. He had arranged for her to have a blood test straightaway.'

Dave and Becky were listening in amazement as Jim spoke. His voice broke and his eyes filled up. There was that same look that Dave had glimpsed on that first night a year ago when they started talking about prayer.

Jim continued, 'Helen was referred to a haematologist and we were told the worse news that we could have had, she had leukaemia. My world fell apart. She was admitted to hospital, but within three weeks she died ... I really do know a little of what it's like to be in the long dark tunnel you're in now,' he added slowly and deliberately. 'I don't know how I survived the following two years. In fact, it only really altered when I met Jo.'

'What did your faith mean to you then?'

'Everything. I learned what it meant to have a High Priest[77] who's been tested in every way like we are, but is without sin. I realised there was nothing wrong in crying; after all, Jesus had done the same.[78] And I realised that suffering is one of the most important means by which God works in us.[79] It's something He uses to make us into the sort of people we should be.'

Just then the door opened. A young doctor walked in. There was a faint smile on his face—it was obvious he was bringing good news!

'Mr and Mrs Knight, I've just come from theatre. We're moving Josh into recovery. He's going to be fine. We had seen a clot that was in danger of going to his brain. We were able to use a new drug that has just come of trials. It has worked wonders. The clot as completely dispersed. It would have been very serious indeed if he had not responded. Nurse will take you down to ICU as soon as he's been moved there. It will be a few days before he can go home.'

Dave immediately turned to Becky and flung his arms around her. He turned to the doctor and, putting his hand out, thanked him. 'Please, please thank all your team! We just can't believe it.'

When the doctor had left, the three friends collapsed on one another as the realisation of what they'd heard sunk in. With arms on each other's shoulders they formed a small circle. They couldn't hold the tears back—they washed the tension out of their hearts.

The door opened again. It was Becky's parents. She ran over to them with her arms out and fell into her mother's arms. They sobbed on each other's shoulders as she repeatedly said, 'He'll be alright, Mammy, he'll be alright.'

The despair had lifted; and, after a while, the five of them were walking up to intensive care unit. They felt they'd been pulled back from the edge of an awful abyss, and feelings of exhilaration and exhaustion coursed through them all.

Then they saw him through a window! Josh! High-tech monitoring equipment was sounding around him and a nurse was repositioning his drip. He was so calm, a picture of how his parents were now beginning to feel.

'Jim,' Dave whispered, 'thanks for being here for us, and not just today.' He grabbed Jim's arm because, at that moment, words failed. But Jim knew what Dave wanted to convey. He smiled at him through his own tears of relief, and slipped away from the family.

As he turned the car into the frozen drive, he could see Sophie's light was still on in her bedroom. 'Poor

Sophie!' he thought, 'still cramming before her chemistry exam tomorrow!' He could see smoke billowing out of the chimney and Jo's silhouette through the lounge curtains. She'd waited up for him, and had kept a good fire going too.

He sat for a few moments in the car, and something Dave had said earlier in the year came into his mind. 'My, it's good to be home!' And it was.

Questions to Ponder

1. Are Christians promised that they will avoid the pressures or tragedies of life?
2. What should the response of Christian friends be when someone is in serious need?
3. Have you ever been in a place where you found that you could not pray? Was there anything that helped you at that time? How did you come out of it—if you have?
4. What did Jim mean when he said that he discovered what Jesus being the Great High Priest meant?

References

[1] Isa. 1:18

[2] Mark 6:4–6

[3] John 5:1–15
[4] Matt. 10:1; Mark 16:15–18
[5] 2 Cor. 12:7–10
[6] 1 Tim. 5:23
[7] 2 Tim. 4:20
[8] Phil. 2:25–30
[9] Rom. 8:18–25; Phil. 3:20–21
[10] Rom. 8.11; 1 Cor. 15:42–44
[11] 1 Tim. 4:10
[12] Acts 16:27–34
[13] James 5:10–11
[14] James 5:8
[15] Rev. 14:13

References

[16] Ps. 128:3
[17] Acts 16:6–10
[18] Acts 13:4-14, 17:1-15; Rom. 1:8; 1 Thess. 1:8–10; Col 1:3–11
[19] Acts 8:26–27
[20] 1 Cor. 7:25
[21] Acts 4:23-30; Rom. 15:30–33; Eph. 1:15–23, 6:18–20; Phil 1:3–11, 4:6–7; Col 1:3–14, 4:2–4; 1 Thess. 1:2–3, 5:16–22; 2 Thess. 1:11–12, 3:1–5; 1 Tim. 2:1–2; Heb. 13:18–21; James 5:12–20
[22] Acts 12:1–17
[23] Mark 6:14–29
[24] Mark 14:32–36, 15:21–41
[25] Acts 7:54–58
[26] Matt 10:16–39, 16:24–25, 20:20–28; Mark 8:31–38; Luke 9:57–62, 12:49–53, 21:12–19; John 12:20–33, 15:18–25
[27] Prov. 3:3–5
[28] 1 Cor. 7:39; 2 Cor. 6:14–18
[29] Matt. 6:33; Eph. 5:16
[30] Prov. 12:15, 19:20; Eph. 5:15–17; 1 Cor. 12:4–6
[31] Phil. 4:6–7; James 1:5

References

[32] John 14:14
[33] Matt. 4:5–6
[34] Matt. 18:19
[35] James 4:3
[36] Mark 11:22–23

[37] Matt. 21:19–20

[38] Mark 11:12–14, 20–21

[39] Mark 11:15–18

[40] Zech. 9:9

[41] Zech. 12:10

[42] Zech. 13:17

References

[43] John 17:9

[44] 1 Tim 2:4; 2 Pet. 3:9

[45] Acts 4:23–31, 16:22–25, 28:28–31; Phil 1:12–14; 1 Peter 4:12–19

[46] Rom. 15:25–27; 1 Cor. 16:1–4

[47] Lev. 19.9; Isa. 17:6

[48] Gen. 41:25–36

[49] Amos 4:1

[50] John 6:5–13

References

[51] 1 Cor. 7:32–35

[52] 1 Tim. 1:15

[53] Heb. 2:16–18, 4:14–18, 10:19–23; 1 John 1:5–2:3

[54] Job 1:8–11; Zech. 3:1; 2 Cor. 2:9–11; Rev. 12:9–10

[55] John 14:25–27; 16:7–11; 2 Cor. 7:8–11

[56] 1 Pet. 3:7

References

[57] 1 Cor. 12:12–31

[58] Eph. 5:30

References

[59] Acts 18:25 AV

[60] Matt. 24:36

[61] 1 Jn. 5:16

[62] 1 Tim. 2:1–3

[63] Luke 10:2

[64] 1 Tim. 5:8

[65] Job 1:5

[66] Matt. 19:13–14

[67] e.g. Matt. 4:23–25; 8:5–13,16; 9:1–8, 18–26; 15:21–28, 17:14–18

[68] Matt. 8:28–34; 9:20–22, 27–30; 20:29–34

[69] Matt. 6:9–13

[70] Rom. 8:26–27

[71] Rom. 8:18–25

[72] Eph. 6:18–20

[73] Rom. 15:30–33; 1 Cor. 1:4–9; 2 Cor. 13:7–9; Phil 1:19–20; Col 1:3–14, 4:2–4; 1 Thess. 5:16–18; 2 Thess. 3:1–5; 1 Tim. 2:1–8; 2 Tim 1:3–7; Philem. 1:4–6

[74] Phil. 1:3–5, 2:17–18

[75] Matt. 5:11–12; 1 Peter 4:12–14

[76] Eph. 6:10–20

References

[77] Heb. 4:14–16

[78] John 11:35; Acts 20:36–38

[79] Rom 5:1–5; 8:28–39; 2 Cor. 1:3–7; 12:7–10; Heb. 12:7–11; James 1:2–4

SD - #0021 - 070726 - C0 - 185/110/7 - PB - 9781912445059 - Gloss Lamination